The Good, The Oops! and the Funny

Enjoy the antics of these kids!

Sally Labadie

The Good, The Oops! and the Funny

Events in the Life of a Teacher

By
Sally Zolkosky Labadie

To order additional copies of this book, contact:
Xlibris Corporation
1-888-795-4274
www.Xlibris.com
Orders@Xlibris.com
60881

Dedicated in memory of my father, Vincent Zolkosky, who inspired me with learning about nature and in sharing it with others; to my son, Ed, who always inspires me; and to my students, who created the memories.

Chapter List

Acknowledgments

With special thanks to the Shiawassee Scribblers for their support and encouragement.

Prologue

"But Mrs. Labadie, WHY are you retiring?" wailed Amber as she roughly back-bumped the heavy entrance doors and then ran down the sidewalk towards home. She never waited for an answer. I had explained to the students in March that I had been a teacher for 32 years, a principal for 5, and I was going to further other goals—to work with teacher interns at the university level, and to be a scientist doing volunteer paleontology.

It was gratifying that despite some wrinkles and a lot of silver hair, the kids didn't see me as old. Sure, I collected fossils, but I wasn't put in that category. To me, it was time to change, and to reflect on those past years.

Thankfully, Gertrude Crampton had required that we keep a journal of our student teaching experiences. Miss Crampton was my seminar instructor at Eastern Michigan University in 1962. She was the author of a picture book, *"The Large and Growly Bear,"* and a bear she was. She was large and had a quiet but growly demeanor. We had many discussions about our daily work, and I still have the journal with her smiley faces and comments.

Although I will admit that at times I didn't keep up the journaling as much as I should have, it still followed me through those many years, and has given me many chuckles and some tears.

And to all my students—while your names may not be in print, you are within this book—in the activities, the learning, the fun, and most of all, the memories.

Sally Zolkosky Labadie

With the exception of my beloved mentors, Mrs. Miller and Mrs. Pearson, college professor Gertrude Crampton, and my own family, names have been changed to protect the identity of the students and teachers.

In The Beginning

Some of the most memorable events of student teaching were not in the classroom, but in getting there. I was placed in the second grade classroom of a three-room school that housed a kindergarten, first and second grade. Begole School had been an "annexed" country school and had never been abandoned because of overcrowding in the city schools.

As a freshman I had had to get a job in order to get through college. My mother helped me get a job as a cashier at an Ann Arbor restaurant, and I rode with her until a car came into the picture. My older brother went into the service and gave his car to my dad. I bought my dad's car, a 1954 Ford. Dad was a truck driver, and his car had been driven like one. It was rough looking and rough riding. My brother-in-law painted it bright blue to cover up some of the rust. He painted it with a brush, so there were little streaks visible in the dull finish. While it wasn't great, it was transportation.

Every day I picked up the other two student teachers for Begole School from a dorm on campus (I was able to live at home), and drove the two miles to the school. When I hear teaching interns today talking about their transportation woes, I let them know that I have been there.

Even before I was student teaching I had some interesting experiences with "Old Blue." Once, while heading to work on busy Washtenaw Avenue, I passed the University of Michigan stadium (on a game day) when all of a sudden my accelerator was stuck to the floor. The car started lurching forward, faster and faster. I put my toe under the pedal to pull it up, and the pedal came off. What's that? A red light! I braked with all my might, fighting against the still roaring motor. As soon as the light changed, I turned down a side street and moved to the side. I put it into park (yes, it was like shifting while doing 60) and turned the engine off. A man stopped behind me, as he sensed a problem, and offered to take me to work. (Wouldn't do that today!) I went to a nearby house and called to leave a message for my father. He came later and fixed the accelerator linkage—a relatively simple fix.

Rust was a growing problem. The fenders flapped as I went down the street, and one evening as I was driving home from my older sister's house a headlight dropped out and hung by the wires. Thankfully, I had haywire in the glove box. Dad always made us carry haywire and in the winter, ashes.

Well, Old Blue was not great, but it got the three of us to work. In a fashion, that is. Every day after leaving the dorm, I had to make a left turn onto a street that immediately went uphill. From a dead stop my Ford could barely get up enough energy to make it up the hill. I think we all were trying to push it in our minds. And then, heaven help me if it was raining! Whenever I accelerated, the wipers stopped. The hill and the wipers were a real problem, the fenders kept flapping and the headlight hung low, but the old blue car kept rolling, and we were never late. So when my college interns have car problems, I certainly can relate!

All three teachers in Begole School had been in the field for years, and had taught in that building from the beginning of time. (Or so it seemed to us.) I think I had the best deal, as Mrs. Miller was the kindest, sweetest lady. She loved the kids dearly and the parents respected her. She knew all the families and even though it was the first day of school, there was a real homey, community feeling.

In order to help me get to know the kids, she had them share something about themselves with me. Raymond told about his pet white mouse. It seems the mouse escaped his cage, and a search of the house produced no results. Then one day his mother unloaded the washing machine, and the poor mouse was found at the bottom—dead, of course. Raymond said that the mouse apparently been in a pile of clothes and had gone through a wash cycle. "But," Raymond drolled, "That mouse was clean clear through."

Raymond handled big words like a pro. We were talking about how big the earth is and how much of it you can see from a plane. Someone suggested viewing it from a ferris wheel. Raymond said, "I was on a ferris wheel once, but I got axaphobia." I had to chuckle, but Mrs. Miller kept a straight face, and asked him what it meant. "Oh, you know—you get sick." And he held his hands to his mouth like he would vomit.

I remember being concerned about Dylan. He was slow in reading, but was a hard worker. He didn't play much with other children—he didn't know how. Apparently he wasn't allowed out of his yard, and other children weren't allowed in. His only associations were at school. Of course, we were limited with totally solving this problem, but it was something I worked on by using small group activities that provided him with a chance to interact with the other students.

Early in the year Mrs. Miller told me that teaching math was my best feature. That floored me, as math was always my worst subject. I tried to make it fun, and maybe that worked for all of us.

I had one little girl, Candice, who had hair so blonde it was almost white. She was a little sweetheart, and was a great student. At that time her father owned a shoe store in downtown Ypsilanti. I hadn't seen her or heard anything about her for many years . . . about 25, to be exact. I went to a dentist in Flint for some specialty dental work, and he had the same last name. I asked him where he was from, and he said he was from Ypsilanti. Well, he was a cousin to Candice, and he also graduated from high school with one of my sisters, who was in middle school when I was doing my student teaching. You really need to behave yourself, because connections are all over!

Children in the early 60's weren't as sophisticated as children of the 90's. When introducing mammals, they were pretty upset when they were told that we were animals. Mary, a top student, was especially disturbed. How different from later years, when even kindergartners recognize our classification.

In late September I wrote about a problem I had with reading. We had four reading groups, and we followed the textbook, word for word. I just couldn't keep the children's attention. The faster children always finished their workbooks first, and then were left in their groups to become mischievous. By October I had started making up questions by myself instead of using the text questions. I gave the children an objective to look for when reading. It worked. Purposeful reading, it is now called.

I loved the middle reading groups. One group had the devilish, crew cut boys with shining eyes who were full of spirit. The girls in the group were sweet and good and yet impish at times. They all were so much fun, even though they kept me on my toes.

Josie was a tiny girl. She reminded us of a caged rat, scurrying from one thing to another and not doing anything. She had problems with her math, and her artwork was done quickly and always looked thrown together. I remember spending a lot of time with her to try to keep her focused. She didn't cause trouble, but we sure worried about her, and I often wonder what happened to her in later years.

Joe was a bright little boy, who was always making noises. One day he wore a new, beaded Indian belt to school, and wanted to share it during "show and tell." He walked to the front of the room, unbuckled it and took it off. He held it up, and as he started to speak, his pants started to slip down. With his free hand he grabbed his pants, held them, and headed for an empty chair in the front, where he sat down and finished his sharing without so much as a missed word.

Interns (student teachers) today still write units. We wrote them as well, complete with objectives. My big unit was on "Indians." One of the art projects was a totem pole made out of cardboard tubes with all kinds of things pasted and colored on them. One of the girls had a face that had two circles, and a slightly larger one, in between and slightly lower. She said it was the "kitchen sink." Yes, she included everything AND the kitchen sink.

We built a "real" tepee in the classroom out of tall sticks and large pieces of burlap. Mrs. Miller brought in a bearskin rug to put inside so when the children went inside to read, they would have a warm, soft rug to sit on. I brought in a large Indian drum I had made out of a nail keg during my industrial art class. I dressed my little sister's three-foot tall doll in Indian clothes, and put it by the drum. We made tiny Indian villages, sang Indian songs and had a wonderful time. And guess what? We did it without textbooks.

Another problem that remains with interns today is time management. I never had time to do things in class, and after school I had to drive the other girls home. Bulletin boards, sorting and checking papers just didn't get done during the day, so I often returned to school to complete work. I also worked at a restaurant nights, so it was a busy year. Time management was tough then, too.

I received a great mid-term evaluation from Mrs. Miller. I remember thinking how it was like a dream. I had gained so much confidence in my teaching I felt very pleased. I credited some of it to my job as a cashier working with all kinds of people.

Worries? Yes, we had plenty. One, I'll call Dorothy. She had been registered at school by a "cousin." She later told us she called him "father" also. She was one of six children, several in foster homes. The previous year she had gone to an "American Legion" school, and we had no records or report cards. She also had gone for a very short time to school in Ann Arbor, and we were told, upon questioning Ann Arbor, that her father was in "the pen" at Jackson. Dorothy told us he was in the hospital. One of her older sisters, a fourth grader, had been taken out of school because she was pregnant. Dorothy was already two years older than our second graders, and her learning was behind. She had no reading skills. Her previous school told us, "Don't worry if you can't teach her anything." We couldn't believe that any school would give that advice. It still frustrates me. Because I was at the school for just one semester I never knew what happened to students like Dorothy, and I have always wondered about them.

I participated in the conferences, just as interns do today, and they went very well. Mrs. Miller had said that the parents usually "clam up" when the student teachers are there, so I didn't need to be at all of them. I participated in those that I attended, and I saw no signs of parents being afraid to talk. One of our parents told me that her son wanted his dad to meet me, because if he (the child) were older, he'd marry me. The father was unable to attend, but his mother, Mrs. Miller and I had a chuckle out of it.

I had my first case of a child vomiting all over her desk and books. Surprisingly, I didn't get sick while cleaning it up. We didn't have a custodian there during the day, so it was "do it yourself." And there were no disposable gloves, either.

Christmas was a great time for me. I am from a large family where it's always busy at holiday time, but this was much better. The excitement of "See my snowman," Christmas presents, a Christmas play, and making decorations just makes Christmas a special time in school. This joy has followed me throughout my career. Every year the kids and I would decorate the room to the hilt. We always had an artificial tree, (which for several years was aluminum), and made zillions of decorations to take home.

That year we made ceramic dishes as gifts for the parents and sent them to the high school to be fired. I had the children glaze them and we all waited anxiously for the finished products. What a surprise! Of course, glazes look different when they're fired, and the kids couldn't believe what they had made. They looked like "glass!" I never forgot this project, and several years later, brought back the messy but rewarding work of creating ceramic gifts.

Tragedy and responsibility: Mrs. Miller was hospitalized with pneumonia, and since she also had heart trouble, she would be out for some time. A sub was hired, but I pretty much ran everything—even the Christmas party. I wrote in my journal:

> "I've never seen so much excitement in a bunch of kids as when we started passing out presents—the squealing and jumping and laughing. I knew I couldn't hold the excitement back so I didn't even try as long as there wasn't chaos in the room. During refreshments they were much calmer, but still excitement ruled the air. I gave the students pencils with the school name on them, and my picture in a homemade folder. They came up and hugged me and thanked me over and over again. I don't think anyone has ever reacted to a gift of mine like they did."

Do you wonder why I went into teaching? I wrote in my journal "What am I ever going to do without these kids?"

Miss Crampton replied, "You'll feel that way about *every* class." And you know, she was right!

Early Years of Teaching

The first years of teaching may be hectic—with learning the curriculum, the culture of the school and the community, and forging relationships within the staff. My very first year of teaching was at Cady School in Wayne, Michigan. It was exciting to get the classroom ready for my second graders. Another new teacher lived across the street from me, so right away we became friends as well as colleagues. Bulletin boards were prepared, supplies set out, and the student list posted on the door, ready for the arrival of the students. I was primed and in top form.

It wasn't long, however, before I became discouraged. The students weren't self-disciplined, and they weren't progressing as fast as I had hoped. I caught one girl cutting her eyelashes with scissors, so I talked to her mother and the principal. I didn't observe that behavior again, but I watched her closely. I learned that you needed to watch all the students every minute they are in your care.

Knowing when to refer a student for testing can cause anxiety. When you question what content is or is not being retained, you need to talk to colleagues, the principal, special education persons in the building—and refer. The referral alone isn't binding, and you'll know more about the child. Andy was a sweet boy, but had obvious learning problems. He had little short-term memory, and I had little experience. I did have enough sense to apply to have him tested for possible special education placement, but unfortunately, I wasn't there to follow through with it.

In the early 1960's it was a common practice for the administration to insist that if a teacher became pregnant, she had to leave by her fifth month of pregnancy. It wasn't a maternity leave, either. I needed to resign because I didn't have tenure. My fiancé and I had been married in June, shortly after my college graduation, and had planned to have a family, but not so soon. However, because I discovered in September that I was pregnant, my day was coming up, and Thanksgiving seemed like an appropriate time to make

18

the break. What a struggle for a new teacher! I wouldn't finish the year with "my" kids. What would happen to them? Of course they would be fine, but emotions seem to overcome reality sometimes. The parents planned a party for me, and presented me with many beautiful baby items.

After my son was born I returned for a visit so the students could see him. I was a little jealous that it wasn't me in that classroom, but life does bring changes.

My first full year was spent in West Allis, Wisconsin, teaching second grade at Walker School. Again, the anticipation was exciting and preparing the room occupied my mind and body, but the room placement was less than perfect. My room was all alone in a hallway just off the parking lot. Directly across from the classroom door was the boiler room, complete with a food-stocked bomb shelter (common in those days). Further down the hall on the left was the gym, and on the right the office. I was physically and emotionally alone.

We had gym class every day, but only one day was with a gym teacher. The other days we were expected to follow a lesson plan set up for us. This class took the place of a morning recess, though I still gave the students a bathroom break. Teaching gym can be intimidating, but the plans weren't difficult; exercises, then a game such as volleyball, relays or working with throwing/catching skills. We didn't have the supplies that gym teachers have today, and some teachers were vocal about having to teach it, but the school policy was enforced.

As a new teacher I struggled with supplementing the regular basal reading program. Since I was basically by myself, I didn't have someone with whom to share ideas with. The principal was upset because I completed the required basals so quickly, but he found me more books to use. His little lecture was that I needed to supplement more. This was difficult for a new teacher who was separated from the rest of the building, but I knew he was right. I didn't have the resources that experienced teachers had, and had no other teachers to talk to. Supposedly there was a reading consultant for the district, but I never met her or had any offers for help. There were no grade-level meetings, no common planning times. The lesson I learned was to go to book sales, gather "freebies," and save, save, save.

My principal taught me another good lesson. One day I was walking my students to the library when he stopped me. He also called to one of my students, "Janice, would you come here?" He then told her to walk toward the library, and told me to look carefully at her. She was walking almost on the sides of her shoes.

"You know, Mrs. Labadie," he explained, "you need to take a good look at these kids and what they wear. This could be a physical problem, or it might be as simple as getting her new shoes." He called Janice's mother, and she had new shoes the next day.

The next year I was teaching in Bloomingdale, Michigan, and was surprised one day when a new student came to school with *no* shoes. She said she had none. After the children left that day, and before I could do anything about it, a local minister's wife (and mother of another of my students) was at the school with a pair of tennis shoes. What an angel! Her concerned daughter had gone home, told her mother about it, and she rushed out and bought a pair. I was thankful for the caring attitude of both mother and daughter. Many years later I worked with a teacher who was proud of the fact that she did not look at what her students wore. She didn't want to become "prejudiced," she said. However, I looked at my students. I wanted to know if they were cared for—or if something was wrong. Mr. Robbins, I always remembered your lesson about looking at the students. I sent him a letter a couple of years after I left his school, thanking him.

"First years" are not only the very first year of teaching. My second year started several days after the school year began. We moved back to Michigan, so my husband, Harold, could start a new job. That very day our new boss told me that if I went to the next town where he lived, in Bloomingdale, I might find a teaching job. I immediately headed to the school (and left Harold to unpack), where they needed to form another fourth grade classroom. I started the next day.

And what new experience did I have? An empty classroom, except for an old upright piano painted white, and a wooden teacher's desk and chair. In piled the students with their books . . . and desks! I had to scrounge for teacher manuals, paper, and all the other supplies. I didn't even have a day to prepare the room . . . but it worked.

I found a mentor, so helpful for any new position. Mrs. Pearson, the other fourth grade teacher and a beloved teacher in the district, became my saving grace. It made me wonder if I would ever be that loved in a school district. It certainly was something to work toward. Mrs. Pearson knew all the families, just as my student teaching supervising teacher, Mrs. Miller, had. That comes with years of being in one district, and it was a blessing for me to have such gracious persons to mentor me.

A new curriculum for a different grade level! That was pretty scary, as well as the fact that many of the students were below grade level. There was a wide gap in abilities—wider than I had had before. There were some very intelligent students, and I didn't want to shortchange them, but I also knew I needed to readjust for those who needed extra help. In reality, all elementary teachers teach several grade levels, and I certainly did that year. I had to search for appropriate reading books and readjust the math assignments. Spelling, social studies and science were easier to adjust, and I took it upon myself to do so. Of course, teachers still have to individualize instruction today, but also they must be mindful of the district and state standards.

It was during these early years that I started a "gab session" with my students. We would gather into a circle and talk about problems at recess, or anything else that needed to be discussed. Today a meeting like that is called a "class meeting." It doesn't matter what it's called, but the students need a time to get their feelings and opinions out. They might also come up with some important solutions.

Weather caused some interesting experiences. During my year in Wisconsin and then after I moved to Bloomingdale, ice was a problem. Two boys, sliding on the ice before school started, fell and broke teeth. The first, Leonard, broke off the top of one of his front teeth when he hit his metal lunch bucket as he fell. Leonard left to get a temporary cap, but Jon, in Bloomingdale, needed a more extensive repair job. He broke both front teeth, and received a pair of temporary silver caps. When he smiled, that silver glistened. I think the family was happy that his school pictures were taken before the accident.

1967 was the year of the big snow. It was early February when, as I was leaving for school, the snow started to fall. By the time we had our first recess at 10:30 it was close to 6 inches deep. School was dismissed early, and it took me a half hour to drive the 5 miles home. We ended up with 2 feet on the level, and with 5 and 6 foot drifts. Everything stopped. School was out for a full week. We lived near a railroad track, and a huge work engine with a snowplow was brought in. Even the trains couldn't cope. Our library roof caved in from the weight of the snow, and snowmobiles became the transportation of choice. I made good use of the free time and baked a lot of valentine cookies for our party at school. The students (and teachers) were eager to return and get back to work, and I know the parents were relieved that the kids were back in school.

Some new beginnings are easier to handle. Three years later, when I moved to Corunna, I found a well-equipped classroom and an overly stocked closet. The previous teacher had taught during the Great Depression, and always ordered more supplies than she needed. I didn't have to order construction paper or tempera paint for years, but I learned that you shouldn't order too much at any time. Construction paper fades after years, and newer, better paint comes on the market. I finally threw the old materials out, but felt guilty about it.

With the help of a new mentor, Nora, a teacher's aide, I was rapidly immersed into the culture of the school and the community. Nora was also the parent of one of my students, and I still enjoy meeting her today, usually in the grocery store. Mentors don't always realize that they not only help the new teacher, but every child that teacher works with.

Another "first" came after teaching 13 years. Jayne, a teacher from another building and I were chosen to be the teachers of a new program for academically gifted and talented students. I was to teach the second and third grades, and she the fourth and fifth. We were to be located in the old, original Corunna school building, which was at that time housing the administrative offices. We were assigned rooms—empty rooms. Not a desk, not a pencil. We scrounged in the storage rooms for tables and chairs and for teachers' desks. We found huge bookshelves in old, unused classrooms on the second floor. In the basement we found wonderful science supplies from the previous science program, which had consisted of "kits" for the different areas. Since we didn't plan on using many textbooks, the few we gathered from the other buildings worked out fine. We were allowed to order some supplies, but since it was almost time for school to start, they arrived after the beginning of school.

We were to write our "own" curriculum, making sure to cover the system objectives. What a great chance to bring in creativity in the arts and to teach content areas across the curriculum. It worked! After two years in the older building we were transferred to Vernon, where I had previously taught. We continued the program for 15 more years, when it changed into a fine arts program for all. A new idea, started with empty classrooms, but filled with eagerness and a true joy for learning, the program was a huge success. Test scores were off the wall, and students went on to be great successes in their chosen fields. "First years" can be rewarding beyond comprehension.

I noticed that over the years I began to teach brighter and brighter children, and they became more creative. However, I came to realize that the reason did not lie solely with the children. My growth as a teacher allowed *me* to become more creative and more responsive to individual children's needs. This should happen to every teacher. You need to continually grow. You should never become a teacher who knows everything and doesn't need to take classes or listen to others' ideas. Yes, you will become more confident and comfortable, but you must recognize how you change. Miss Crampton, my seminar professor at college was right. In 1962 she said that I would find every class better and better. But she didn't say why.

Read Alouds

Reading to the students was always important to me. I wanted the students to love reading, and also wanted to introduce them to topics and learn about history from books that they might not pick up by themselves.

I remember that as a girl I disliked biographies. As an adult, I realized the contribution they make to literature as well as to the study of history. My students loved hearing and reading about Helen Keller, Daniel Boone, Florence Nightingale, and Albert Einstein. I read a book to them about Charles Stienmetz, the "father" of G.E., and then I explained about his life. How enraptured they were, but they were also concerned that people made fun of the hunchbacked genius.

I also showed a filmstrip (boy, does that date me) about the life of Stephen A. Douglass. The students would blurt out "It isn't fair!" when it told of segregation policies of the old south.

I wrote in my journal,

> "I do believe I have succeeded in making them more aware and concerned for the feelings of other human beings. I only hope they retain this compassion."

One year, as Thanksgiving was nearing, I was reading the Pilgrim story to the students. On a bulletin board I had placed a large cutout view of the Mayflower, and wrote the caption, "The Pilgrims were crowded on this small ship." After we had talked about the lack of bathroom facilities and how the Pilgrims couldn't wash their clothes, second grader Charlie asked how come I didn't put a "y" on "smelly" on the bulletin board. When he explained what he meant, I realized that all the time the picture was up, he thought the caption said " . . . this smelly ship." The book brought the Pilgrim story alive for the students, in more ways than one.

My fourth graders back in the 60's hadn't read *Charlotte's Web*, (and it wasn't yet made into a movie), so that was chosen as an important book to read orally. Being a highly rural area, and familiar with animals, the students were enraptured by it. When I came to the part where Wilbur tried to spin a web by having a string attached to his tail and jumping off the manure pile, the students howled with laughter. It was so uproarious that I had to stop reading for at least 5 minutes, because I was laughing as hard as they were. I never had a class react like that to the story before or after that. The background of your audience sure makes a difference.

One year I decided to start an "Invention Convention" with the students. We read *The Twenty-One Balloons* and enjoyed the creative inventions in the text. This led the students to create their own inventions and to hold an Invention Convention for the parents. During our second year of creative inventions, I invited other classes to join in the activities, and after our own convention we participated in a countywide convention. The students were proud of their ideas, such as an automatic bedspread roller, a hat grabber, a fitted blanket, and a fork especially made for catching the syrup when eating pancakes. And all because of the influence of a book.

Over the years probably the books most loved by me and by the students were the Laura Ingalls Wilder books. I had been introduced to them when I was a third grader in school, and started reading them to my own students. When I taught in Bloomingdale, my mentor teacher showed me a letter that her students had received from Laura several years before she died. I was almost a little jealous because I wouldn't have that opportunity to correspond with her.

The "Little House" books were a great lead-in for a celebration of Heritage Day, and some of the items I collected to display were similar to the ones in the books. One year I packed up my niece, Anne Marie, and her friend Connie, and drove to Mansfield, Missouri to visit Laura's home. I purchased pictures, a replica of Ma's china shepherdess, replicas of Laura's rag doll, Charlotte, and of her sister's china-head doll. We visited the home and museum and drove to the cemetery to see the graves of Laura, Almanzo and their daughter, Rose. Some years later I visited DeSmet, South Dakota, where the surveyor's cabin and Ma and Pa's home is located. I drove to the cemetery there to see the graves of Ma, Pa, and the other family members, as well as those of other persons in the books. The cottonwood trees that Pa planted were still growing near the spot where their homestead cabin once stood. Seeing all of these places from Laura's life made her feel like a sister to me. She was very real, and when I read the books the students felt that way too. One group of students decided to make name cards like Laura did when she was young. They decorated little cards, put their names on them, and passed them out. I still have several in one of my photograph albums.

One year I was integrating some special needs students into my "gifted" classroom. My students were very accepting of the new members of the class, and considered them as our own classmates. The special needs students in turn felt welcome and participated freely in our discussions and activities. I was reading the book *Farmer Boy*, the book about Almanzo, Laura's husband. Little Kathy was in my room to hear the story. While I had third graders, she was only in the first grade, but older than a regular first grader. Kathy loved the story, and knew that if the students had the book they could follow along with me. She went to the librarian and asked for the book with "cows on the front." Jean, the librarian, didn't know what she meant, but asked her why she needed it. Kathy told her that I was reading the book to the students. Knowing that I was reading the Little House series, she went to the shelf and looked at all the books. And there was *Farmer Boy*, with two young oxen on the cover. Kathy was thrilled. As I read to the students she had her book open. I went to show her where I was in the story, but she didn't want me to show her. She wasn't on the right page and couldn't read the words, but she didn't care. She felt like she was reading, so I left her alone so she could "read." Her smile was all the reward I needed.

When I was taking classes to receive my administrative certification in 1993, I was in a class of three other administrative hopefuls. Of course, I was the most "mature." Then there was Beverly, who had only taught three years. Pat had taught more, and was in her late thirties. Lyla was a little older. Lyla and I would walk to our cars together after the class. We formed an instant bond. Her son had recently been in a minor automobile accident, and since I had gone through an even more serious one, we had something in common.

After our final exam we all went to a local pub for dinner with the professor. After we ate, I took out one of my teaching journals from the early 70s. Beverly had been complaining that there were no rewards in teaching. Oddly enough, the week before that last class meeting, I had had two visitors. One, the stepparent of a former student, Bart, told about Bart's accidental death and how much influence I had had on him in the few months he was in my classroom. The other was Ray, a student in the same class as Bart, who was, indeed, a boy who was not afraid to get into trouble, but whom I enjoyed. Ray just "stopped to visit," showed up on his Harley, complete with long hair and leather jacket. I took the journal to read to Beverly about the days with those boys and to tell her how there truly are rewards, though they may not be apparent to you at the time.

As I started to read, Lyla grabbed my arm and asked, "Did you always teach in Corunna?"

I was caught off guard, and thought, "What is this?" However, I just said, "No, I taught a year in Wisconsin. I taught four years before moving to Corunna."

"Did you ever teach in Bloomingdale?" she persisted.

I was floored. How did she know? Bloomingdale is a very small town on the western side of the state. "Yes," I managed. "I taught in Bloomingdale for three years. Do you know someone in Bloomingdale?" I later thought that that was a stupid question on my part.

Still holding my arm, she excitedly said, "You were my fourth grade teacher. And you and Mrs. A were the reasons I went into teaching!" I might add that it was over 30 years previous to this experience.

Rewards? What greater example than that. But what does that have to do with reading to the children?

My professor asked her what it was that made her, after 15 weeks of class, to finally realize who I was. You see, in our class we went by first names, and I now had grey hair and had long ago shed the cat-eyed, plastic-rimmed glasses.

"Her reading to us. She read to us every day. And I still read the Laura Ingalls Wilder books to my students. When she started to read, I recognized her."

The visual of seeing me read, and the auditory sense of how my voice changed when I read, had turned on the light for her.

On the last day of school one year I found a note on my desk. It read;

> Mrs. Labadie
> I know we've had problems but you've taught us a lot about life.
> And all's well that ends. Well, it's our last.

The note was signed by all the students in the class.

Where the message may not make sense to the reader, it meant something to me. In reading the Laura Ingalls Wilder books to the students, they heard how Laura's Ma frequently said, after some disaster, "All's well that ends well." And in one of the books a humorous incident was told about the death of a shoemaker. After he died, people said he "gave his **awl**" and others said that it was "his **last**."

And so, the students remembered. Somewhat. And tears still come to my eyes upon reading those words.

Another incident came up many years after a student left my classroom. C.J. was a quiet boy—so quiet and shy that his first book reports had to be given to me privately because he couldn't talk to the class. According to his mother, he had been humiliated by the teachers as well as the students at his previous school because of his shyness. By the time he finished two years (second and third grades) with me and two years with my teaching partner, Jayne, he was a different boy. He was outgoing and well liked. The family moved away, and I heard nothing about him until one day in 1999 when my sister from Grand Rapids told me that my niece, who sang in the Folk Choir at Notre Dame University, was coming to Grand Rapids, and I needed to be there. Apparently another choir member at the college was talking to my niece, Ann Marie, and mentioned that he was from Michigan—Corunna, in fact. Anne Marie said that her aunt taught in Corunna. When she told him my name, C.J. was surprised. He said, "No way! She was my favorite teacher!" Well, I did go to the concert, and there he was. He looked the same—only more mature and handsome, of course. The singers called him "Wild Man" because he played the bongo drums with wild exuberance. He asked me if I still read *Eddie and Gardenia* to the students. I was pleased that he remembered the book, and was able to tell him that I had just introduced it to a third grade class that very week.

We usually don't know how those stories connect with the students, and it is rewarding to hear of their impact—even if it is 12 or 13 years later—or even 30.

Those New-Fangled Machines

Copy Machines

When I first started teaching, students had workbooks for almost every subject. Once in a while you needed to make copies of something to reinforce learning that went beyond the workbooks, and dittos were used. To make a "ditto," also called a "mimeograph," you needed to type or write on a special paper that had a sheet of carbon paper behind it. The carbon went onto the back of the sheet you were writing on, and when you put it on the roller of the ditto machine, a special ink covered the print and made copies. If you made a mistake you had to use a razor blade to scratch the carbon from the sheet. The ink had a strong smell, and you usually ended up with blue hands from the combination of ink and carbon. Needless to say, I didn't use dittos a lot.

When budgets were tight it was recommended that we use copies (made on the ditto machine) instead of workbooks. Some publishing companies sold books of carbon "masters" that could be used with the workbooks, but we sometimes used them in place of workbooks. The masters would be good for a couple of years, but the carbon eventually wore off and the copies became dim and sometimes smeared.

When copy machines were introduced we were in heaven. Workbooks became a thing of the past and books that were legal to copy were purchased. It was so easy that some teachers became "ditto queens," giving their students dittos for everything from reading to art. Schools today often put limits on how many copies each teacher can make because toner for the machines and paper is so expensive. I used copies when necessary, but my students learned without the reams of dittos. They were happy without the busy work, and I was happy I didn't have to check all the unnecessary papers.

During one of our big presidential elections I was standing in a long line to vote. I was bored, and said to a friend near me, "I wish I had brought some papers to check."

A lady a short distance ahead of me turned and said, "When you've taught as long as I have, you learn to just throw them away."

My mouth must have dropped, and when I regained my composure, I asked her where she taught. She was in an elementary building in the neighboring city. I said no more. I couldn't believe that a teacher would have her students spend time doing work just to have it thrown in the wastebasket. It was quite a few years later that one of our own teachers confided in me that she often threw papers away. This, to me, was an ethical problem. In my opinion, every paper must be recognized, if even with just a smiley face or an O.K. I think it's a problem brought about by our easy access to copy machines.

Films

In college we had to take an industrial arts class where we learned how to "thread" a film projector. It wasn't difficult, and I used the skill for several years. When I moved to Corunna there was a "new" automatic-winding film projector. It was so easy! You just needed to stick one end of the film in, and around and around it went. Some of the older teachers refused to use the "newfangled" projector. I found it fascinating, and the students loved to watch it threading around the knobs and gears all by itself.

Then came the day of the videos. I started taping nature shows at home and using them to supplement science. They were up to date and the photography was excellent. Shows on volcanoes showed colorful explosions and the ocean reefs were alive with beauty. The Intermediate School District (which later became the RESD) had the older films available for loan, but videos were easy and inexpensive to provide by oneself, so the loaner films became obsolete.

When I was taking the industrial arts class, I had been told that television was the "wave of the future" in teaching. Every student had to create a show that was shown on a classroom monitor as if it were being presented to many schools. I had a pet rabbit, and created a show about the care of rabbits. That was in 1961. Televisions are now extensively used, but in very different ways.

For me the use of television in the classroom started in 1968 when I moved to Corunna. Michigan State University had several TV programs for children during the day. There was a music program, and a new show called *Electric Company* was great for teaching phonics. Bill Cosby hosted the show, and humor was used throughout. One day the characters were using "er, ur, and ir" sounds. A little boy appeared with a piece of chalk and a brick wall. He looked around sneakily, and asked, "Do you want to see a dirty word?" My students were glued to the TV. He wrote, "A dirty word." The entire room cracked up. I learned how effective it was to play with words by watching this show, and over the years I continued to use humor from the show to help students relax and enjoy phonics and writing in general.

Our school had televisions mounted on huge steel bases that could be moved from room to room. One year a TV fell off the base onto a student. She wasn't seriously hurt, but we soon had straps to hold the sets on. Storing the huge monsters was a task in itself—the storage rooms were small, and often they were packed full. Gradually, in the '90s, the parent teacher organizations started purchasing televisions that were then mounted on the wall of each classroom.

These TVs are now used to show school news broadcasts, videos, and DVDs as well as demonstrating computer use and to present PowerPoint programs. It took many years, but televisions are now appropriately renamed "monitors."

However, television monitors may be heading out the door soon, thanks to the advancements in computers, overhead projectors, SMARTBoards and document cameras, which project everything to a white board or screen. Even DVDs or movie clips can be run through computers and onto screens. I know of several schools where wall monitors are being removed. That's progress.

Laminating

For years teachers have been decorating their rooms with beautiful pictures, and in the '60s companies started creating figures to put up that were made of light, colorful cardboard. A problem was that the tape or thumbtacks used to hold them tore the posters and figures, and they soon became raggedy. In 1969 our school system purchased a heat press that would laminate small items. It was only about 18 inches square, so the size of the job was limited. It was useful only for small items, but we still used it whenever we could.

In the middle '70s, my teaching partner, Jayne, showed me a laminating machine at the Genesee Intermediate School District building. We could laminate large items for a nominal fee. We would pack up our materials and head for Flint. When we came home, we each had a huge roll of laminated items that made the expense of buying the decorations and posters well worth it.

Elsa Meyer had been a former principal, and one of the elementary buildings was named after her. In her will she left some money for use in the elementary buildings, and I was on a committee to decide what to purchase. A big item was a portable stage that allowed us to dispose of an old rickety wooden one. The stage has lasted many years, and is still in use today, although with new, more formal skirting around it.

The other item was a laminating machine. Thanks to my fellow teacher's idea, it was just like the one we had used in Flint. It was housed in the central office, and everyone could use it. The machine was used and used and used. Finally, every building purchased their own, and they are still indispensable.

Computers

Many, many years ago, when I was a senior in high school, I was the first one in my typing class to be allowed to use our brand new electric typewriter, which was the first for the district. I remember how everyone crowded around me to watch its operation. The machine responded to a very light touch and automatically moved to another line. No more hitting a return carriage. It was easy to use, but I never dreamed that by the time I would retire, electric typewriters would be obsolete, and computers would run our lives.

In the early 1980s our school had some demonstration models of the TRS-80 computer, which utilized cassette tapes for the memory. We found them difficult to operate and limited in their performance. In 1983 I joined a new technology team for our school district, and we visited the Intermediate School District to look at what was out there for schools. We found that Apple (at that time) had more programs for students, so we went with the Apple IIe and bought several for each building. Also on display at the ISD was the new, innovative, Macintosh, complete with a "mouse." This was the coming thing, we were told.

We all tried to draw with the mouse, but I had a difficult time making my hand do what I wanted to see on the screen. Our principal laughed at me, and I guess I did look silly. However, I learned something. I never was good at playing piano as a child, or on the French horn, which I played in high school. I had always had a difficult time with manipulating things. On that day it dawned on me. I did not have good eye-hand coordination. It hadn't been because I was dumb or anything, but I had never thought of any other reasons. Talk about taking a long time to learn. And it made me think of what we do to students who have motor control problems.

I bought an Apple IIe for my home so I could do all my writing on it. I thought it was a miracle! We saved everything on floppy disks, and I felt like an "expert." That wasn't the general feeling with other teachers, however. Some refused to touch a computer, even after classes were offered.

Several years later the school district purchased an Apple 575 for each classroom, complete with a mouse. The machines were more powerful and gave us more options. Small computer labs were set up in the libraries, but some teachers still refused to consider using them.

My students loved to use the programs. I purchased a program on dinosaurs and one on geography. The students also learned to do word processing and enjoyed writing their own stories on them. What an improvement over the IIe. And we thought the IIe was fantastic!

Andrew was a quiet, but intense student who was drawn to the computer. His father, Dan, was our high school math teacher, and was also learning not only how to use the computer, but how to teach in a computer lab. It was ironic that many years later when I was principal, I was given a new PC for my office. Andrew, now a high school senior, was helping the computer "gurus" set them up, and he showed me how to use it. And I had once taught him how to use an Apple II e! The school finally went to using PCs, and every teacher was required to use them. I am pleased to say that all the teachers I knew finally came to use computers regularly. However, It had taken over 10 years to see that all the teachers in our school district were computer literate.

Overhead Projectors

When overhead projectors were new, one was purchased for the Nellie Reed building. As a new teacher in the building, I found it stuffed in the storage room on a desk especially made so you could sit down and write on the projector while facing the class. I took it to my room, where it stayed until I left the building many years later.

It seems that no one wanted to use it, or couldn't see the use in it. It was well used in my classroom, where the students were fascinated by it. Gradually, over the years more teachers asked to have one. When I was principal I bought one for every classroom. They became an essential part of the teaching process.

Overhead projectors did have disadvantages, however, in that some teachers wrote directly on the glass, and then would squirt water on the hot surface to clean it. Every machine had a transparency roll, but I guess that was too much trouble. Several teachers had the bulbs blow, and one teacher who had put the water directly on the hot glass had the glass break. It was an expensive lesson.

One question remains . . . why did it take so long for the teachers to accept this? I moved to Corunna in 1968, and became principal in 2000. Why did it take so long to learn to use something so simple? I might add here that document cameras are now making the overhead projector outdated. The camera is more versatile, and material such as pages from a book, pictures, or even science experiments can be projected onto a screen. They are a combination of overhead and opaque projectors.

Opaque projectors would show materials that were not transparent. You would insert your picture (or book) onto a tray and move the tray close to the light. The fan was loud, and the light very strong. If you left your material in the machine too long it would warp from the heat. When the fan stopped working, the light would blow out. Needless to say, we didn't use it a lot. The new document cameras are a real blessing. They replace both the overhead and the opaque projectors.

Hands-on Strategies
that Really Work

Heritage Days

Community celebrations also bring about learning in the schools. The village of Vernon announced they would be celebrating their centennial. What an opportunity to bring in a day of fun called "Heritage Day." We selected a day and notified parents well in advance, so if they chose to put together some old-fashioned clothing for their children, they would have time to do so.

I had participated in a centennial a couple of years earlier when I taught in Bloomingdale. We lived in Gobles, another small town, and both Harold and I participated in organizing the celebration, so I had a dress and some experience in organizing displays of antiques. My students loved to hear the Laura Ingalls Wilder books, so they were on their way to an exciting day that sounded like "Laura." To create interest in the other classrooms, I put items in the school showcase. There was a kerosene lamp, old books, a flatiron, horseshoes, and a very long hatpin, to name a few. The grandmother of one of my student's was an antique hound, and filled the library with interesting items. Every classroom took turns viewing a spinning wheel, a butter churn, a "slop jar," a baby cradle, and old toys.

Bob was highly creative and often very humorous. This came out on one of our special heritage days when I took in my usual assortment of antiques, which now included a chamber pot (slop jar). After having the students try to guess what it was used for, and getting the usual responses of "to cook soup in," and "as a salad bowl," I told them its real use. And, as usual, they cracked up. Imagine having to go to the bathroom in a bowl. "Well," Bob said, "at least it's not as bad as doing it in a cup!" When I questioned what he meant, he went on to explain how you needed to do that when you go to the doctor. Need I say more?

My students cooked hasty pudding and made butter to put on homemade bread. Hasty pudding is really corn meal mush, but the students didn't need to hear that. We ate ours with a little brown sugar (which would be similar to the sugar the pioneers used). They enjoyed it so much there was never any left over.

The Heritage Day often brought different displays—from antique bathtubs and kitchen tools to farm implements. One year we had a parent (who was a farrier) demonstrate the trade of horseshoeing—without the horse. A community member brought in a spinning wheel and demonstrated spinning wool, and talked about spinning dog hair. One teacher had her children make ice cream. It didn't work, so she made some at home and brought it in. The students were just as happy with it the next day.

When I visited the Laura Ingalls Wilder home in Missouri, I brought back many photographs and a slide show of Laura's childhood days. These, along with items that I collected over the years became important parts of our special days. I always dressed in an old-fashioned dress when I presented the Laura items, whether it was on a heritage day or not.

In fact, one year on heritage day, I wore my special pink pioneer dress when a student from another classroom came up to me and asked, "Isn't that the same dress you wore two years ago?" When she heard my affirmative answer, she asked, "Don't you ever outgrow your clothes?"

I smiled, and thought to myself, "Do I tell her I've worn this dress for 10 years? Naah!

Outdoor Studies

When, in 1986, the opportunity arose for my students to develop a nature trail, it wasn't in my personality to say no. I had always taught about nature, though not necessarily through the required school curriculum.

In Bloomingdale a wooded area was nearby, so on an early April day in 1966 my fourth graders and I took a hike. I had notified the parents ahead of time so everyone could wear old clothes, and that was a blessing. There was a meadow and swamp along with the woods, where we could find early spring plants popping up and just enjoy being in nature. We jumped brooks, got caught in low-growing thorn apple trees, ran down the huge hills, walked on fallen trees, and sprawled on the grass to rest. What fun! It was nice just to let the students be "kids." My hands and legs were scratched, my nylons torn, and I was exhausted. But it was really worth it. Maybe I never grew up.

Later, when I taught in Vernon, my students planted shrubs and trees around the school. While the shrubs are gone, there are four trees—three red maples and a sugar maple, all growing tall because of my students. For my retirement from Corunna the administration gave me a gift certificate for a tree, so I purchased an oak tree and planted it in front of the building where I worked as principal. It looks like my students and I will be around for a long time.

One year my students went to the local YMCA camp for an end-of-the-year picnic. They were able to use the archery range, walk the trails, and roll down a big grassy hill. This same camp would be used years later when we had a family work bee at our nature trail. But on that occasion we used the canoes and paddled down the Shiawassee River. That was the second time we were on the river. The first came when we were studying river systems and how they affect the settlement and growth of cities. That year we rented canoes and put them in the water by a bridge on Kerby Road. We canoed down the meandering river to Corunna, just above the dam. One of the students lived near the landing spot, and we took videos of all the students passing by. That fantastic trip was followed by a picnic at the city park. I might add that every student not only wore a life jacket, but was accompanied by a parent—a necessary safety precaution.

Corunna High School is located next to the Shiawassee River, and the advanced placement biology class created a nature trail in an area between the school and the river. The first year we used the trail we went on a tour with the high school students, and I decided that the next year we would go out early, before the students worked on it, to see animals and early plant growth.

At that time I was teaching the gifted and talented self-contained second and third grade classrooms in the old high school building in the center of Corunna. It was within walking distance of our building, so we took off. We saw the May apple coming up, spotted a pair of pheasants and a deer. Dennis was hilarious, letting us know about every bug or toad that he spotted. At one point, it looked like he was picking a weed, and I reminded him not to pick anything. He said, in a frustrated tone, "Pick it? It's picking me!" It was true. Nothing had been done on the trail since the previous fall, so pickers and burdocks were all over. When we came out of the trail, I was covered with stick-tights. Carol was right behind me, and her white sweater was covered brown dots. We stopped and took off as many as we could, but what a picture we made, everyone covered with brown stick-tights and burs. We decided, however, that it was worth it, because we wouldn't have seen the animals after the high school students had been working in the area.

Our Own Trail

I had become acquainted with Bill and Pat, who lived near the Nellie Reed building. Pats's mother, Mary, had been a teacher and lived on the family farm about three fourths of a mile from the school. When Bill retired from his job as a detective in Detroit, they moved to the farm and Mary moved to a trailer on the property. For several years I would walk with my students to the farm and Bill would press apple cider for us. The students helped cut the apples and squeeze the press. They loved the sweet, fresh cider, and the bugs getting into the open-air press didn't seem to matter. Even Mary would get involved with the project.

In 1985 I heard of an environmental contest for students sponsored by the state's Natural Resources Department, called the Governor's Environmental Youth Awards Competition, and the wheels started churning in my head. We often had class discussions about projects as well as problems, so I posed the question of entering the competition. The answer was a resounding "Yes!" As for what to do, someone suggested a nature trail. They were all in agreement, but I wasn't so sure of a place for a trail. We were located in a residential area of a small town, with not even a farmer's field closer than Bill and Pat's. Since the students knew them, I said I would check with them to see if they knew of a place.

That very afternoon I paid a call on Pat. As I neared her place, I glanced at some woods across from her home that I had visited a few years previous when I was conducting a breeding bird survey for the Audubon Society. The woods, about an acre and a half, were surrounded on the north and east sides by crops, on the south side by the gravel road, and the west by a grassy hill. I remembered that I had seen warblers and indigo buntings as well as many downy and hairy woodpeckers.

Pat and I sat down for coffee, and I posed the question to her. Did she know about anyone who had a small area that we could adopt for a nature trail? And, did she know who owned the woods across the road? As luck would have it, she told me that she owned the property, and she would be glad to let us use it. I suggested she call her insurance person to check into liability, and I would call the school to check on ours.

Before I announced it to the students I called the superintendent and after he checked with the school lawyer, he said, "Go for it." I don't know who was happier, the students or me. The walk we started then was only a beginning to an almost six year journey.

We had to walk the three-fourths mile to the woods, past the local cemetery and across an old iron bridge that spanned the Shiawassee River. Just across the bridge the road made a sharp right turn, so I painted two wooden sawhorses orange and white and attached a sign that said, "Caution. Children Walking." Every time we walked to the trail I put them up on the road—one in front of Pat's home and one near the cemetery. I also took extra precautions to make sure no cars were coming around the curve before I'd let the students cross the bridge.

Every spring as we passed the cemetery, we'd find the first spring beauty flowers growing on some graves near the road. The mausoleum was painted white, and the students always referred to it as the "White House." Near the mausoleum was an old World War I cannon. And every year the students would duck and hold their breath when they walked past the mausoleum. I thought it had something to do with the interments there, but one year while I was chuckling about it, I asked why. They had always ducked because the cannon might shoot them, and they held their breath because they were afraid of the dead people in the building. The third graders always passed the tradition on to the second graders, so the practice persisted until the final year. And that final year I ducked with them.

I called the local energy company, and they dropped off a huge load of wood chips for the path. I applied for and received a mini-grant through the Corunna Educational Foundation to purchase hand lenses, field guides, and a wood burning set for signs. We then made a list of what we needed to do.

1. Identify plants in the different seasons.
2. Clean up the junk. Many years previous it had been a family dump site. There were bottles, cans and farm waste such as old wire fencing lying among the trees.
3. Identify animals in the different seasons.
4. Plan trails where we would cause little disturbance of natural growth.
5. Create the trails with wood chips.
6. Plan a trail guide.
7. Make signs.
8. Write thank you letters to helpful persons
9. Build nesting boxes for bluebirds and wood ducks.

That year on our annual trip to press cider we stopped to visit the area and come up with ideas. We had a bonus that day when Pat let the students go into the barn to collect chicken eggs. A new experience, and not one egg was broken!

After a few cool, rainy days we had a streak of nice weather, so we headed for the area. We saw a female hairy woodpecker, which stayed in plain sight and hammered at a tree so all of the students could see her. We then saw a downy woodpecker, a nuthatch, many goldfinches, and of course, doves. We worked for about an hour collecting tree leaves for identification and checking out spiders and the frogs in the swampy area.

Some days at noon I would take a few students to the woods in my car, just to see what was there. (Be assured that as times have changed, I wouldn't do it today.) One day on the quick trip we spotted a screech owl. He sat on a branch among some greenbrier and watched us with one open eye. On our way out we saw that he was still there, not 10 feet from us.

One spring day we had a planting party and set about 25 little pine trees on the slope to the west of the woodlot. Stakes were put in to keep track of them. This slope was not tilled because there would be too much soil run-off in rainy weather. The trees were to help prevent the soil erosion. Today those little pine trees are huge and form a regular pine forest.

We had help doing just about everything from Pat and her dog, Iggy. Iggy was an old, longhaired sheep dog who loved the kids. He always found us while we were on our jaunts, and the students thought he was great.

In November the Black family and several students came to work on a Saturday. We took a load of junk to the landfill. The landfill owners were kind enough to let us dispose of everything at no cost. We also moved some wood chips to the entrance. Dan Black had brought his motor home, so we had hot chocolate and hot dogs for lunch. I believe one of the benefits of the nature area was the relationships with the families. On many occasions we had sisters and brothers, mothers and fathers helping out.

I created a short slide program about the trail and had the students create an identification book with pictures and lists of the many kinds of life we had observed. They came in over the summer to create the book telling about our observations, and Andrew painted a beautiful cover for it. The book was sent to the DNR.

In January we received a notice from the DNR that we had won the regional award for the development of the trail. A representative came to the school and presented us with a plaque at an all-school assembly. Of course, Pat was there, and she was very proud.

Word was sent that we had received a mini-grant from the school Educational Foundation, and a check came from the parents of one of my former students. They had heard of the project, and wanted to be a part. How things come together!

We never went to the trail during hunting season, and during the winter walking the narrow gravel (and often unplowed) road was dangerous, so additional work had to wait until spring.

A huge Saturday workday was scheduled in late spring, when entire families came to work on the trail. The Blacks again brought their motor home for a base, and we had trucks and trailers to haul junk away. We found bottles, cans, rolls of fencing and parts of farm implements. In all, we had six truckloads and one trailer load to take to the landfill. And yes, Iggy helped sniff out the junk. This was indeed a community project, as again we were allowed to dump free of charge. The students also spread chips on the trail, using large plastic bags and wheelbarrows to carry them in. Some parents built benches out of upright logs and old boards, and student-made signs were placed to identify trees. A large sign that read "Vernon Nature Trail, 1986" was made by a parent and placed at the entrance.

After the clean up session we drove to the YMCA camp where we had a picnic and enjoyed a canoe ride on the Shiawassee River. What a wonderful experience! The students saw turtles sunning themselves on partially submerged logs. We saw snakes and frogs. Any larger animals were alert enough to hear the excited chatter of children, and stayed away. The students rolled down the hills and explored the woods, eagerly comparing it to "ours." It was one of the best family picnics I experienced in all my years of teaching.

In early September we discussed having an official opening of the trail. I told the students how businesses often have ribbon cutting ceremonies to celebrate a grand opening. I suggested that we have a "branch cutting" ceremony, and they loved the idea. Then I broke the news about having a little speech from one of them. The first one to volunteer was Jenny. She said that she would think up something to say. Jenny was a quiet girl, and it impressed me that she had the courage to do the official speech.

On September 9, 1988, we wore our new, official Vernon Nature Trail shirts that were designed by the grandfather of the Black children, and invited my partner teacher's class to walk with us for the ceremony. There were two newspaper reporters to record the event. I had put a small branch across the beginning of the trail, and Jenny gave her short speech about how they had worked hard and were happy to open the trail. We had a pair of branch cutters for her and it took all the energy she had, but she snipped the branch and everyone applauded.

So now we were official. The students were so proud to take other classes to the trail and tell them about the things we had seen. Over the years we took many classes there, and my students served as the guides.

We built wood duck boxes from precut pieces sent by the Saginaw Valley Waterfowlers, an organization that a student's father belonged to. Susan and Luke's dads helped the students build them, and we set them up on the trail. We knew ducks had been in them, because we often found pieces of shells on the floor of the woods, but more often we saw our little screech owl looking out the door of one of them. One late winter one of the fathers and I met at the trail to clean the boxes. We wanted to make it ready with new wood chips for the ducks in the spring. John cleaned one, and gave me several owl pellets that he found. The owl was in the second box, and he did not want to vacate it. He put my camera at the top of the box and took some great pictures. He then closed the box and decided he'd clean it later. The following Monday the students and I cut open several of the pellets. Sure enough, there were tiny bones and gray fur from mice and shrews. We never realized what neat things we would get into by having the trail.

Later in the year John returned during the week when the entire class was there, and opened the box that was the owl's home. He forced the owl out and the students got to see him fly off. The box was then cleaned and readied for the ducks. My husband then built a more appropriate "owl" box, but it was readily occupied by a mother squirrel and her babies.

We were invited to a neighboring school to speak about the trail. The school was going to start their own nature area, and wanted to see what we had done. We put together a slide program and took a bus ride to Shaftsburg. We wore our trail shirts and using the slides, the students talked about the process of creating the trail. We were then taken on a walk in their outdoor area, and had refreshments with the other students. That school built a beautiful area, and it is still used today.

There was a summer that the weather was hot and dry, and the poison ivy proliferated. I hated to resort to spraying, but I needed to protect the children. Several times that summer I attacked the dangerous plant with vengeance. Once I was heading in with the heavy sprayer in hand, when I heard a cracking sound, like branches breaking. I dropped to my knees and looked where I thought it came from. Sure enough, there was a doe, with not just one, but triplet fawns. I watched them for about five minutes until a car came around the bend in the road, did a 360, and roared off. The deer were startled and ran off across the field.

There were times when I headed to the trail at noon by myself. One of those times I spotted a flock of sandpipers in a pool of water in the neighboring field. They were migrants, but it was exciting. I stopped as soon as I saw them, turned the car around, went back to school and gathered up a few students so they could see them.

Another trip found three students with me on a trip after a snow. We saw a crow soaring down toward the snowy field, and as we looked we saw a mouse scurrying across the white expanse. The crow was heading for the mouse. My car must have scared him off, because he rose suddenly and flew off. The mouse found safety under the snow by a large tree, and the students were elated at the narrow escape.

Helpful Parent John went to clean out the boxes one spring just prior to a big work day, and found the boxes full of wood duck eggs. The planned work day was postponed to let them hatch. The following week, with some of my students acting as guides, we took another class to the trail and a hen flew out. It was exciting for all of us to see, and especially to the other students, who had very little background in nature studies.

Every year we made the trail our goal for our end-of-the-year school picnic. One year we took cardboard and walked to a nearby abandoned gravel pit so the students could slide down the slopes. We often walked an old railroad bed nearby and picked (and ate) wild strawberries. On one picnic walk, we recorded that we sighted an indigo bunting, our resident brown thrasher (he loved to chatter at us from the top of a dead tree), bank swallows and catbirds. We often saw a kingfisher as we crossed the old iron bridge that spanned the Shiawassee

River, and the kids thought it looked like he had a Mohawk haircut. At the gravel pit we saw footprints of deer, raccoons, small birds and herons.

When I moved to the position as principal, our trail days came to an end. I was in a different building nine miles away, and it just wasn't possible to continue. Bill and Pat later sold the farm and moved out of state.

A few years later a new teacher, Randy, was hired for the Nellie Reed building. Randy had worked at a nature center and was very interested in science and the outdoors. I talked to him to see if he was interested in continuing the project, and he thought he might give it a go. I stopped to talk to the new owner's mother, who had a store in the next town. I had had her daughter in school, and her son also had been a Vernon student. I asked her if she would check with him about using the area again. She did, and he was all for it. I gave Randy the good news, and he and I met there to look it over.

I was amazed at how tall our tiny pine trees on the hill had grown, but I was somewhat discouraged by the woods itself. Storms had knocked down trees and branches, and the place looked in worse shape than when we had started . . . except it wasn't full of old junk. He had his work cut out for him. I created a photo album of our work for the school as a historical record.

With the state pressures of testing and new curriculum guidelines, Randy can't spend the time in the woods like we did, but he does take his students there, and that means something to me. More students are learning to appreciate the outdoors—and to understand the ways of nature. And all because my students and their parents said "Yes!" to a new idea.

Young Authors

I was introduced to Young Authors' Day when my class was located at the old Shiawassee Street building. For those two years we "connected" with Elsa Meyer School, and traveled there for gym class and lunch. They were holding their annual Young Authors' Day, so we were invited to join in the fun.

All of the students were to publish a book during the year. The students wrote a story, and parents (or as in my case, I did the work) typed the story onto blank sheets. The students then illustrated the pages and the finished pages were bound into a book format with a plastic binder. It was a time-consuming job, but the end products were beautiful, and the students were very proud.

A special day in May was set aside for a celebration. The day started with a production by the staff. The teachers selected one book and made it into a little play. Humor was always included, and the students howled with laughter. One year the male principal dressed up as a little girl, and one of the younger male teachers was a dog. He even raised his leg when he went out the door. Another play had the male special education teacher dressed as a longhaired cheerleader.

When one of my third grader's books was chosen, we had teachers acting like dinosaurs, chasing other teachers who were pretending to be boys who had built a time machine. What a hoot! The author of the book was always the narrator, and it was a very special time for them. But the question is, who had more fun—the staff or the students?

In a later year, the principal played Abe Lincoln, and I played Susan, one of my students. For variety, we asked a student to play me, as I was the teacher in the story. In the story I (Susan) imagined that Lincoln, in a picture on the wall, winked at me, and because I insisted that I saw it, I was sent to the office by the teacher. It was funny and enlightening to me, to see how the student represented me. Was I really like that?

One of the teachers thought I did a fantastic job with my portrayal of Susan. She said that "inside of me was a rebel and an actor." Actor, yes. We teachers are always on stage when we teach. Rebel? Probably. I have always been quietly rebellious, as the reader may realize.

The students were often put into small groups of mixed ages, with a parent or community volunteer as a leader, where they read their books. Guest readers were invited into the schools during the week to read their favorite stories.

Over the years the celebration evolved into a day where many kinds of activities were held. Animals were often there for display and/or petting, the Sheriff's Department brought their police dog, and the fire department bought a truck the children could sit in. There were demonstrations on hair care, as well as arts and crafts. In later years I also brought in reject material from a phosphate mine and had the students look for shark teeth.

My teaching partner, Jayne, and I took the book publishing and celebration idea to the Nellie Reed building when our program was moved there. We decorated the entire school and hung flag banners outside. It was such a lot of work that it evolved into a semi-annual event. I usually alternated it with Heritage Day.

When I moved to the Elsa Meyer as principal, we continued the semi-annual practice, and I purchased banners for the hallway. In more recent years the special day has been continued, but decorating has been eliminated. One addition, however, is a cookout. The school district purchased large grills and transports them to the individual buildings one day every spring, when the administrators cook hamburgers and hot dogs for everyone. The cookout has been held on Young Authors' Day and the presenters and guests are invited to the feast.

To give the occasion a different flavor, one year the staff decided to have each class study a different county, and use the theme of the country in decorating. Julie had a Scottish background, so had a major role in helping our class decide on Scotland. It was also perfect for me because of my Scottish heritage. We made posters of Nessie, a castle, a map of Scotland, a Shetland pony, a Scottie dog, and a bagpiper to put in the hall. My brother Bill made us shortbread (a specialty for him) and Jennifer's mom helped me make scones for brunch. Yes, we made them in the classroom. I brought in teacups and we had a very Scottish tea party.

Julie's uncle came in to speak to the class. He wore a kilt, sporran, tam, and the entire regalia that he had purchased on a trip to Scotland to work on family genealogy. I wore a suit in my family plaid, a blouse from Scotland, and a wool tam. What a fun way to study a different country.

In some years special authors have come in to talk to the students as a motivation to writing their own books. Often they bring their books to sell and autograph them for anyone who purchases them.

And how did the students' books change over the years? When we first started, teachers and parents typed the words onto blank sheets. When computers came into the picture, my students typed the words, cut them out and pasted them onto a 6X9 blank sheet. The students decorated the covers and we usually laminated them. The entire book was bound with a plastic spiral binder. This worked beautifully, until "blank books" were discovered. These are blank pages bound by a blank cover. The students either used cut and paste for the words or wrote the words themselves directly onto the pages. They then illustrated the pages as well as the cover. The parent teacher groups were always generous in purchasing these books, and the students had a beautifully finished "real" book to keep. I still think I had as much fun helping the students write and publish their books as the students did. The time and energy put forth was well worth it.

Publishing children's stories doesn't need to be restricted to a special day. I have "booklets" that were made using the old ditto machines that contain student stories, poems and illustrations. The booklets were made for the parents, but the main idea is that the students have an audience. My first booklet was from my first year of teaching in Wisconsin, and continued for several years. I gradually matured into a more refined book of bird poems, for example. Each student wrote a poem and illustrated their own page. The poems often were sent to the local newspaper for their children's page, or left in the school library for others to read. I was impressed that the idea of "publishing" a book carried over into social studies and science. When students studied an area such as the Devonian period in our "dinosaur" unit, or Native Americans of the prairies, they needed to share their learning with the rest of the class. Some groups created books. The binding machine in the teachers' workroom was put to good use.

Curriculum

"New" Ideas in Science

When Corunna instituted a curriculum council, I was asked to chair the third grade team. We met monthly, looked at new textbooks and talked over classroom happenings. One year we examined various methods of teaching science, and decided that a hands-on approach was needed. We took a field trip to Michigan State University, where two "kits" were demonstrated. We decided on the one that seemed to suit our needs, but for some reason, received the other. It consisted of many huge boxes of materials, mostly consumable.

My son, being in the same building as I was, didn't think much of the kits. His comment was, "Some science! They don't tell you anything you don't already know. It's no kit, just a bunch of junk they threw together. Where do teachers get all these ideas, anyway?" He never had a teacher who used these kits appropriately, but because he was a very hands-on boy, he would have thrived. These particular kits, while having many good materials, had many items that were of no interest to some teachers, and weren't used correctly to help the students "discover" scientific principles. We used these kits for several years and then discarded them. Probably the biggest problem was that there was no person or money to replace the consumable items, to make sure batteries were good, or to replace broken materials. One weakness in the kits was that there was no natural science. It was all magnets, lights, colors and electricity.

We returned to science books, which I used only as a resource. I had always taught science by observation and investigations, and I continued to teach that way until I retired. The main drawback was that many other teachers used the textbook—totally, and without investigations. They also taught only what they liked. One teacher decided she didn't like to teach about electricity—so she didn't. Another didn't like life sciences, so she didn't teach it. Many years later, with the implementation of district and grade level objectives, and the "threat" of failure with the Michigan Educational Assessment Program, this changed. This was one of the few positives results of statewide testing.

A good example of hands-on learning was when I spotted some Tinkertoys left together after an indoor recess. They were fitted together, and a rubber band was placed around them like a pulley. When I came back from lunch I found Robby finishing his creation. It amounted to a lot of gears and pulleys, and by turning a handle, worked two spiked pieces at one end. He called it his "eggbeater." Years later Robby went on to become a master mechanic and welder. Talk about skills for life!

In 1993 the school district brought in a professor from Michigan State University to teach a science lesson using the conceptual science approach. Innovative? He taught a science lesson without a text, using a hands-on, discovery approach. Jayne, my teaching partner in the gifted and talented program, and I had done that for years! I was more than a little frustrated because our principal apparently thought we teachers were too limited to be able to teach that way.

The lesson was using the discovery approach, like the kit program we had used years ago. I had liked it. It was great-except most teachers didn't want to take the time to gather materials and get set up. Some didn't *have* time and some wouldn't *take* the time. I always felt that a science resource person would be a tremendous help, but financially that was out of the picture. What happened after the demonstration from MSU? Most teachers went back to their texts, and Jayne and I continued our hands-on teaching. Maybe the principal was right. Maybe many teachers were too limited (but probably were just too lazy, didn't have the knowledge, or they felt too insecure) to use the method.

I always tried to integrate other subjects into science. For ten years I was at the opposite end of the hallway from a sink, but we still did papier mache dinosaurs, created pots of plants for mother's day, and used paint a lot. In studying geology we listened to the *Grand Canyon Suite*, read *Brighty of the Grand Canyon*, learned how to blend chalk to make a picture, and then used the chalk to make pictures of canyons. There were no art teachers, and integrating the projects just seemed sensible. I passed out a recipe for "Grand Canyon Jell-O," and Josh made some for the entire class. The participation and spontaneity of the students was out of this world.

Parent Conferences

How do you improve or change parent conferences? In 1993 I investigated student-directed conferences, and decided I wanted to try them with my third graders. The students made portfolios of completed work, and they helped make out their own report cards. They decided what they were good at and where they needed most help. I stressed the fact that papers saved must include all levels of grades, because if they saved only the A papers, their parents would assume they didn't need any help.

Mark and Alice helped me model a conference for the rest of the class. They were to play the part of the parents, and I took the role of the student. After I had presented my work to my "parents," Mark patted my arm and said, "We are so proud of you, little Sally."

The conferences were highly successful. The students were prepared and the parents were amazed. They never realized that their children knew so much about their own strengths and weaknesses. When a child said, "Mom and Dad, I need you to help me with multiplication," there was a greater impact than if I had said it.

When I became principal, several teachers tried it and were impressed with the results. However, because it took work and organization on their part, the practice dwindled. There are teachers in other schools who use forms of this conferencing, and who tout its effectiveness.

Reading

The grade level groups met to look at new reading books. Each building had previously been able to use whatever they wanted. There was no continuity, no sharing of books when one building received more students. We were asked to select a series that would be used district-wide. The teachers griped and argued about the books and about having to coordinate, but we finally settled on one company's series. That is, except for two teachers who were furious because the books were not "traditional" enough.

I had been in their classrooms, and all the students' artwork was the same—no creativity. The students had to use patterns and dittos. The rooms were neat as a pin, with no exciting, interesting materials for exploration. Those teachers would not admit that their "traditional" approaches might not be effective in a changing world. I was outspoken, and said that it was time to start something new and refreshing. We were scheduled to start the new science kits and a new reading text would prove to be time-consuming on our part. But if the students learn, isn't it worth it?

Most elementary classrooms taught reading using reading groups. Yes, I utilized this method, with adaptations for individuals. In those days the groups were usually named—like the "robins." I never named my groups, but instead just used the title of the book to identify a group. Why try to "hide" book or group levels I thought. The students never complained, and neither did the parents.

We often had fun plays during reading time. One year a group of students asked if they could use the play *Hansel and Gretel*, which was in their reading book, to present to the class. Of course I agreed. They read the play, assigned parts, created simple costumes and a few props all by themselves. The day

48 | Sally Zolkosky Labadie

of the play came. Dennis lay on the floor by the wall the entire time, not participating in the actual play, but from time to time he would raise his arms, shake them, and put them back by his side. We all laughed at this display, even though we didn't understand what the object was. When the play was over, I asked him what part he was playing, and his answer was, "The witch's dead husband." They had had one student too many for the parts, so Dennis had created his own role. Creative?

Another time we were reading the *Pied Piper of Hamlin*, and I asked what we would call a man who could do the kinds of magic tricks that would make a hill open to let the children in. I expected the term "magician," but John called out, "A kidnapper." Yes, John. I guess you were right.

Reading groups were usually brought to the front of the classroom where the students gathered around a table. Even though we had chairs around the table, the scraping and banging of getting ready and leaving the group drove me up the wall and distracted the students working at their desks. My father solved the problem by talking to a carpet distributor who supplied the store where he worked. He brought an entire carload of carpet samples to donate to our cause. I taped some together in a bright, alternating color pattern to put on the floor to create a library corner, a first in our building.

I had a supply of carpet pieces at the front of the room, and when the students would come up to a reading group, they would just take a carpet to sit on. No more scraping, banging noise! It was heaven.

The students wrote thank you letters to my father and Mr. Brown, who donated them. Janice wrote, "Dear Mr. Brown. Thank you for the carpets. We shit (sit) on them while reading."

Because I created many of my own lessons, the students put together their own "workbooks." I needed a spot to keep them where they were organized, and where the students had easy access. They already had so many things in their desks that I needed to create a new space. My husband built me a set of shelves using bi-fold doors, and it fit perfectly along the wall under the windows. The students collected their booklets, and I told them to put them on the top shelf, in neat stacks, one for each row. Dennis turned to Lydia and said, "That's because Mrs. Labadie likes it neat and she's well stacked." I stepped outside the classroom door, leaned my head against the lockers, and counted to 10. I never told Dennis that I overheard his comment, and I wondered if Lydia understood it. I firmly believed Dennis knew what he was saying—but he was wrong. I was never "well stacked."

During the years Jayne and I taught the program for the Interested and Talented students, we taught reading using novels. Most of my novels were either biographies or historical fiction, thus hitting more than one content area.

We taught book clubs and literature circles long before they were named. It just took creativity and a lot of free books acquired when the students purchase books from Scholastic.

Spelling, writing and literature is all put together today and called "literacy," so I'll put in a few words about spelling.

Teaching two grades created some thinking about giving spelling tests. I solved it by giving five words for the second graders, then five for the third, and so on. It worked very well, and also provided time for some creativity from Martha. She wrote side comments on her test paper.

asparagus—yummy—not
grimace—what you do when you eat asparagus
diaphragm—near where the asparagus goes
abominable—asparagus
fricassee—fry, fry a hen

Would you allow these kinds of comments? To me it showed that Martha understood what the words meant, and I still chuckle at her comments.

Today even first graders receive spelling tests. Years ago they didn't. The first exposure to a spelling test came in second grade, and my classroom at this time was a combination room with regular second and third graders. These little guys were pretty naïve when it came to tests, and Charlie, on the very first test of the year, tried to solve a problem. The word was "mother" and he didn't know how to spell it. So, he turned to his neighbor, and asked out loud, "How do you spell mother?" The third graders laughed, and so did he, when he realized what he had done.

Fifth grader Betty almost stumped me during a spelling test. "Number 10—enunciate." I said. Betty asked, "What?" I repeated it. Several more students caught on and asked "What?" I was going to repeat it again, when I realized what was up. I laughed and said, "Am I not **enunciating** properly?" It was their turn to laugh. I was glad they had learned what the word meant! They also felt comfortable to explore and have fun learning.

When I was principal, I made it a habit to walk through every classroom every day or two. A fourth grade teacher was dictating spelling words for the week as she wrote them on the board. A girl raised her hand just as I walked by. I bent over, and asked her if I could help her. She said, "No, it's a teacher question." I assured her that I had been a teacher, so she informed me that the words all have the same vowel sound. Apparently the teacher hadn't mentioned it, and she figured it out. I told her that she was right. I think I was qualified to listen to that comment.

Social Studies

When I moved to Corunna in 1968, I found out that the third grade social studies was taught using the most boring text I had ever seen. In third grade we were to teach about the community and community workers. It reminded me of teaching that a town had "a butcher, a baker and a candlestick maker." Those ideas were assuming that the students were unaware of the kinds of stores located in their town. Even in 1968 the students were more sophisticated than that. I skimmed the book with the students and brought in some interesting activities—research and map making. I rarely used the text, but covered the same material. Sara was a new teacher across the hall and in 1972 (her first year) my son was in her classroom. I had always tried to allow him to be like any other student. If the teacher wanted to talk to me about him, I was there. I didn't want to always be on his case. One day as I took my students to gym class, I noticed him sitting in the hall. I walked on, not saying anything. Later that day, Sara came to me and said she had caught him reading a comic book behind his social studies book. She saw this but didn't let him know she had seen it. She called on him several times, trying to catch him unaware. However, he always knew the answers and where they were in the text. And that was what aggravated her. I talked to him later, telling him that I fully understood how he felt because I had to use the same text. (I didn't stress how I supplemented it.) However, I insisted he had to follow along as the teacher asked. In actuality, I couldn't blame him for being bored. And Sara, being a new teacher, was really doing her best.

I was pleased when we, as a grade level team, looked at new social studies texts. Some were still very traditional, but one was much more worldly. It brought in communities from the past and from other parts of the world. The Mayans were highlighted, as well as ancient Zimbabwe, even before Rhodesia became Zimbabwe. All this before studying prehistoric cultures became "in." The company had filmstrips, tapes, and additional brochures that showed Mayan art and the ruins at both Zimbabwe and Tikal.

As expected, the more traditional teachers complained. They didn't want us to mention other parts of the world. They wanted us to continue to study the local community through third grade. They didn't see the growth towards a global community. What was the outcome? The really interesting text was adopted, much to my satisfaction.

The students enjoyed the prehistoric cultures, even though the parents sometimes misunderstood—or were uninformed of the places we were talking about. One child said that his father told him there was no such place as Zimbabwe. We were just ahead of the times.

When learning about the number system used in the ancient city of Zimbabwe, the children were surprised to find that they used their hands and individual fingers as a base in counting. Gene burst out, "Did they have the naughty finger in those days?" It was as easy for some children's minds to wander in the '70s as it is today.

When reading to the students I often chose books on a topic we were learning about. Cathy was a dark-haired, blue-eyed beauty. When she was into a story, she could be very intense. I was reading the story of Daniel Boone, and came to the part where the British wanted to incite the Indians to distract the revolutionary troops. I stopped briefly and explained the tactic. Cathy came out with a serious, "Gosh, I hope we win!"

"Yes, we did," I answered her, "Two hundred years ago."

Happily, she said, "Good!" It was as if it were happening that day to her.

The children loved to write reports. They enjoyed the research and did their best to write their reports on the computer. Bob was researching Henry Ford. He and William were looking at a picture of Ford's first car. Seeing no steering wheel, William asked how they steered it. I explained that the stick (lever) was used to steer. "Oh," he replied. "A joystick!" How our vocabulary changes with each generation.

When I taught fourth and fifth grade, we taught about our constitutional rights and personal responsibilities. I had had these students for three years, so they knew me and weren't hesitant to discuss things that they might not bring up in another classroom. We were sitting on our "discussion carpet" one day, talking about "freedom of the press." We bantered back and forth on the rights of the press, and of their responsibility to report the news factually. There had recently been reports in all the papers of a lady who had cut off her husband's penis. Obviously, this was on Bert's mind when we talked about reporting.

He broke into the discussion with, "Did you hear about the lady who cut off her husband's . . ."

"That's enough!" I said quickly, with all the students laughing at the idea. But, we did talk about how it was reported. And talking about how much needed to be stated in the paper, someone said, "The papers even told where she threw it." They thought that was hilarious. After talking about whether that was a necessary item to print, we had to wash up for lunch. As the students washed their hands, Linda came up to me and said, "Mrs. Labadie, if she cut off his penis, how could he go to the bathroom?"

I said in a matter of fact tone of voice, "It's okay, because they sewed it back on." That brought down the house. After laughing with the students, I stood quietly, and they knew it was time to quit.

Mark added, "Oh, yeah. We need to quiet down because we're role models for the little kids." And they did. And they were.

One time we were talking about the lumbering industry and all the different products that were made from wood. Someone suggested "material" (meaning fabric), so we briefly discussed how different fabrics were made, and nylon really interested them. I told them it was made of coal tar, petroleum and agriculture by-products. Toni, bless her, said she "thought nylons would be awfully heavy with all that stuff in them."

Judy's parents had visited Australia, so Judy brought in a video of the trip that included her mother shearing sheep. In this video her mom worried about hurting the sheep during the shearing process. Judy complained, half laughingly, "My mother was so worried she'd cut the sheep, but she doesn't worry when she cuts OUR hair!"

The video also had an aborigine playing a digery doo while others were dancing. The kids were so impressed with this dancing, which included bouncing up and down, that they tried it at school and at home. They gave up quickly when they found they just couldn't bounce like the aborigines. The thing that stuck with me was the old song, *Tie Me Kangaroo Down, Boys*, which was played on the video. I think I heard that song in my mind for days.

Handwriting

When I started teaching second grade I experienced the frustration the students go through when moving into cursive writing. Jimmy was having trouble making a cursive "e." He tried and tried, and finally said loudly, "It doesn't work!"

I walked over to him and showed him again how to make it. "Now that's a good e," he said confidently. He went to work again, and yes, it worked!

I had always taught handwriting using the old ball and stick method. When our gifted and talented program brought in students from the neighboring school district, I quickly realized that their second graders had learned with the newer D'Nealian method. I didn't want to change them at that point, so I had to hustle to learn more about it. Besides teaching two grade levels, this meant another addition. I had some second graders using the traditional method, and the two new students using this new way. I soon found it was a beautiful method of writing, and very practical. When the second graders made the transition into cursive, the flow was easier than I had ever experienced. Because I fell in love with the style, I worked with the curriculum council to allow me to pilot the D'Nealian method for the next year. The next year our building became a pilot, and then the entire district adopted it, and it still is in practice today. I encouraged my students to try new things—don't be afraid. Dare to be different! We teachers need to be role models with trying new ideas.

Critters in the Classroom

"Critters" always had a place in my classroom. Through the following examples one can see the excitement they created as well as how they provided children the chance to love and care for something alive, and at times to grieve over those that die.

Bugs seemed to be always present. During my first year of teaching in Wayne, Michigan, a student brought in a beautiful cecropia caterpillar. I had her take it to show the secretary, who told her it was just an old tomato worm. The girl came back almost in tears. I reassured her that it wasn't just a tomato worm. I showed her a picture and then hustled to the office, where I told the secretary how upset the girl was. The secretary reiterated that it was a "Wayne" tomato worm. I then informed her that my parents had had a produce farm in Wayne when I was little, and I had picked "Wayne" tomato worms by the dozens. I showed her the picture of the cecropia moth and caterpillar, and she was surprised. Lesson? Make sure you have many resource books so you can identify all the critters brought in.

One year we had a preying mantis egg sac hatch. What fun it was to look at the tiny creatures under a magnifying glass. They were just like the adult, but so very small. We had to gather them up and let them go, or they would have invaded the entire school. Feeding adult mantises was a great activity. We often created makeshift cages and the students would collect crickets and grasshoppers at recess. It also helped give the students something worthwhile to do outside, and there were few playground disputes.

And thinking of a preying mantis, one year my sister brought me a HUGE one that was five inches long, and had a brown body. My husband made a wire enclosure for it, and for a week it feasted on grasshoppers and crickets found by eager children. They were all disappointed when I took it home to release it, but that disappointment was quickly forgotten when Mary brought in another "critter."

Mary brought a spider in a jar, and the students enjoyed putting insects in for it to eat. It didn't eat, but created an egg sac. We left the jar at school to see what would happen, and in two weeks we had tiny brown spiders by the dozens. You might guess, the jar was promptly sent home.

While reading *Charlotte's Web*, I had many spiders brought in, from tiny ones to a preserved tarantula in a jar. I had learned my lesson with spiders, so those were enjoyed only for a day.

I scrounged up a microscope so we could look at the critters more closely. The students responded by bringing in over 75 (I counted them) caterpillars, spiders, sawflies, pinch-bugs and moths.

One year, after having a "buggy" classroom, we wrote insect poems and illustrated them to be put into a book. Jacob brought his page up to show me. His illustrations and poem were all centered at the top of the page. I questioned why he had left such a large blank space at the bottom. His comment? "Oh, that's where the sewer is!"

Snakes and turtles regularly showed up in my room, and sometimes they wandered there by themselves. Somehow, they would escape other classrooms and find their way under our door. Or, as in the case of a turtle, wander the halls until someone found it. One time a custodian put one in my terrarium because he "assumed" it belonged to me. Another time I found one in my desk drawer, put there by another custodian so I would find it. It helps to have many jars and a terrarium handy for unexpected visitors. At that time, I wrote in my journal,

"Holy snakes and jumping turtles! What will happen in the room next?"

What will happen? Talking about snakes, a large garter snake once lived in a terrarium in our classroom. Kate brought in two frogs one day and asked if she could put them in with the snake, which she had also brought. I made sure she understood what would happen, and she seemed okay with it. It wasn't long before someone screamed. Of course, a frog was being eaten. It caused such a ruckus that I put a jacket over the terrarium until the frog was gone.

The same snake decided to take a little trip when we were at lunch. My student teacher, Charles, and I searched for it—all the while hoping the other would find it! Finally, I spotted it coiled between our stacked reading chairs. A fifth grade boy was handy, and he picked it up and took it outside. After that, snakes joined spiders in being allowed in the classroom for only one day. However, I do still have a snakeskin that is always a big hit in classrooms.

One evening I received a call from an obviously distraught custodian, who asked, "Is there supposed to be a snake on the floor in your classroom?" I told him that I didn't have any at that time.

"Well," he said, "there's one in your room right now." I quickly thought about other rooms, and remembered that the teacher across the hall had two baby garter snakes. I told the custodian to put it in the terrarium in that classroom. He wasn't going to touch it, but found someone who would. I assume that the little snake had exited under the one door and entered under my classroom door. I hadn't known that the poor custodian was petrified of snakes, even a very small garter snake.

I have had students bring in their pets-Sandra brought in her miniature goats, and others brought in their dogs. One student brought a calf, thankfully on a special day when we had other animals outside for the kids to see. Another student whose parents had dairy cattle said that he was going to name a calf after me. What an honor!

Martha's mother was a veterinarian who took advantage of her occupation, and brought in the uterus of a dog. Surgery had been necessary to save the life of the mother dog, so she showed the class how the fetuses are each in their own little sac, and what they looked like at that stage of development. That was a new experience for me as well as for the students.

Mary had talked about a neighbor who was raising some abandoned baby squirrels. One day she brought in a shoebox tied with a string so it wouldn't come open. She brought it to my desk, and told me to open it. I smiled, and asked, "Is it alive?" which was a standard question of mine when surprises are presented. She looked at me, started crying and managed to say, "No." I almost wilted. She was so upset. I opened it, and inside was a dead baby squirrel. "I'm so sorry," I said as I hugged her. But then—what do I do with it? I asked her if she wanted to show the class, and tearfully she said, "No, I just wanted you to see it." I closed the box, tied the string, and let her know I was sorry about it, but glad that she shared it with me. We put it in my closet, where it stayed until she took it home that afternoon. It was with mixed emotions that I contemplated the incident. Sad for her—but I was pleased that she shared it with me. She just wanted someone to know about it.

I once confiscated a dead crayfish (which, thankfully, was dried out and didn't smell) from Michael. Michael wanted to be a minister, and I still wonder about him—had he achieved his goal? And did he remember the crayfish? Yes, I returned it to him at the end of the day. It was his! It was interesting though, that when I took the crayfish out of my drawer, Michael spotted a lot of other student "junk." "It looks like that's Devon's stuff," he said. He was right. I was always taking some odds and ends from Devon.

Sometimes there are unexpected and unwelcome visitors. When I taught in an older classroom in Bloomingdale, mice would die inside the walls. The stench would be strong for a couple of days and then fade out. Nothing would cover the smell. Once I managed to discourage one of the "guests." It was an end of the semester workday, and I was busy figuring grades at my desk when I heard a soft scraping sound coming from the coatroom area, which was located at one side of the classroom. I walked to the area and continued hearing the sound coming from the "scrap box," which was filled with discarded but useable pieces of construction paper, located on a low shelf.

I gingerly moved some pieces and a little mouse jumped out and ran out the classroom door. I grabbed the broom and followed him. He scurried into the small entry—way and out through the open outside door. (Why the door was open in the middle of the winter, I can't remember.) Following him, I swung the broom at him over and over, around the building and to the back where the windows were located. We had two new portable classrooms, which in those days didn't have much of a foundation, and I didn't want him to get under the rooms. I chased him around and over snow piles, swinging mightily, and finally beat him into oblivion. Of course, the teachers in the other classrooms, viewing the sight through their windows, thought I had really lost my mind.

Classroom pets became important to me and to the students. A fellow teacher had purchased an albino guinea pig, and because of allergies, couldn't keep it. Knowing my love for animals, I gave in to temptation. We named him Squeaky, because that's what he did. The students were thrilled with "Squeaky," and they willingly took turns cleaning his cage. They loved wrapping him up in a towel and setting him on their desks while they worked. Wrapping him up served two purposes. It kept him from wiggling and getting loose, and from dropping "pellets" on the desks. Occasionally he would chew the edge of a student's paper, and it was a mark to be proud of. I had a second cage at home, so every Friday I wrapped him up and put him on the seat beside me. He was good about staying calm on the drive home. I didn't want him to be alone for two days. I have observed classroom pets that are left alone on weekends or holidays, and to this day I feel sorry for the lonely little critters.

Squeaky even had his picture in the local paper—on the front page, and in color! The picture was labeled "This Little Pig goes to School." For almost five years Squeaky was our best friend. To show the benefit of a class pet, let me tell you about a friend who had a son in first grade. First grade is a difficult year for many children because it involves going to school all day and being away from mom. Tommy was no exception. Early in the year he came into the building in tears every morning. I spotted him one day and took him to my classroom. I wrapped up good old Squeaky, and let Tommy hold and pet him. I made it a routine for one of my students to bring Tommy to the room directly from the bus so he could hold Squeaky. After a couple weeks of this, it wasn't so difficult to come to school any more. Tommy just needed a little reassurance that everything was fine, and Squeaky did the trick. The psychological comfort that the pig provided was irreplaceable. And what happened to Tommy? He is now a teacher!

One year just before Mother's Day, I found a card on my desk. It had a picture of "me" on the front, complete with brown hair and eye shadow. It read, "To Mom, with love," on the outside. On the inside it said, "From your cute little son, Squeaky." Our attitude toward animals shows through to the children, and they knew I loved Squeaky.

After Squeaky passed into "guinea pig heaven," as one mother called it, we had Ragamuffin, a longhaired black guinea pig, Milo, and Zippy, another white one. Zippy didn't do so well. Late in the first year in the classroom he bit a student, so he became my pet at home. Biting is a big worry with pets, and one must be cautious with the children handling them.

Milo was a calico, and was so tiny when I bought her that she escaped through the bars of the cage. She ran a mile a minute—thus his name, "Milo." All of the guinea pigs were loved and cared for by the children. Except for Zippy, they were gentle and could be easily carried around.

We tried fish and hermit crabs, but be forewarned. They are more difficult to take care of than guinea pigs, and more expensive. I had to come in on holidays to feed them, to clean the tank, and make sure the motor and heater were operating properly. At least the students could clean a guinea pig cage! Fish die easily, and algae grows quickly. Crabs also require a lot of care and are touchy to handle. They bite, and can't be taught not to.

I had a pet Cochin chicken at home, and I regularly took Wooster to school to visit. He would ride on the car seat, hop out and follow me into the building. I had a cage for him during the day, and he would follow the children outside at recess to eat the grasshoppers and crickets they'd find. He had a personality that wouldn't quit, and wanted to be with me all the time whether it was riding the lawnmower or going to the post office.

And thinking of fowl, Andrea started something that followed me throughout my career. Andrea was a kindergarten teacher, and every year she hatched chickens in her classroom. One year she had bad luck. She tried goose eggs, but they rotted. She decided to give it up, so she gave me the incubator. Every year after that I hatched chickens, quail, or ducks. I used a large box with a shop light as a "brooder coop." It was just the right height that the students could reach in to pick the babies up to hold. Chickens take three weeks to incubate, and one year I didn't check the hatching date against the school calendar. They were scheduled to hatch on the last day of our Metropolitan Achievement Tests.

The incubator sat at the front of the room because that was the only free electrical outlet. Jeff also sat at the front of the room because he was hyper and needed constant redirecting. The morning of the last day the chicks were pecking through and peeping softly. During the last portion of the test the peeping grew louder, and one chick was obviously going to break through. Jeff could hardly contain himself. He had finished his test, but needed to stay quiet so the other children could finish. I stood in front of the incubator, and shielded it from his view, but Jeff tried to move and wiggle around in his seat so he could see. Finally I was able to say, "Time is up. Put your pencils down." I ended it with, "Now you can come up to see the chicks." I moved aside and just as the children settled on the floor in front of the incubator, the chick popped out. The chorus of "oohs" and "aaahs" and gleeful shouts made it perfect. What timing! What luck! Suggestion? Watch the dates carefully when starting the incubation.

Some years we hatched ducklings. The students loved them because a couple of days after hatching I would bring in a wading pool and let them swim. The most shocking thing for the students was that as soon as the little ducks were put in the warm water, they'd poop. And then, being curious, and not really knowing what it was, they would pick at it. That seemed to gross out some of the kids.

Both chicks and ducklings were fun to put outside on the grass. The students would sit in a circle and the babies were in the center. They would pick at the grass and run around, much to the delight of the students.

While we were in the process of hatching chicks one year, Taylor brought in a "hawk's" egg that he wanted to put in the incubator. He said he found it on the grass near his home. Since I knew he lived near the river, I told him it was probably a mallard duck, but he was adamant it was a hawk. After the chicks were hatched I took the incubator and the lone "hawk" egg home. About two weeks later, out came a cute little mallard "hawk." I called Taylor and he was disappointed. It seemed he believed that by wishing, the egg would become whatever he wanted.

"Ducky" followed me all over at home and school. The students delighted when he raced down the hall after me. I became his adopted mother, but he actually followed anyone who was handy.

One of my former students lived near the river, and his mother enjoyed watching the wild ducks. We gave Ducky to her and he followed her around until he grew up and flew south to become a wild duck.

I always had a source to get the chicken and duck eggs and made sure I had a home for the babies when they were ready to leave. The students were sorry to see them go, but after a couple of weeks it was time. The ducks were the smelliest! We always changed the paper in the large box at least twice a day for the chicks, and several times for the ducks. But was it worth it? Absolutely.

I must mention that we always named our hatchlings. There was Big Mouth, Corunna (of course, he was black and yellow, the school colors), Huey, Dewey and Louie, (they looked alike,) and Big Bird. Raymond, a visitor from another classroom, announced, "And you're (meaning me) the mother!" One year we had an Early Bird, Chick a Dee, Chick a Doo, and Last Minute Charlie. I had to help Charlie out of the egg, and he seemed okay, except his wastes kept sticking to his rear end. This caused the other chicks to pick on him. I took him to the vet (thank goodness the vet understood our classroom!) and she applied Vaseline to his rear. That did it. He was fine.

We had many discussions about birth and birth defects when a chick or duckling would die before making it out, or when I needed to help open the shell. The children could easily connect it to their own lives and they began to understand why human babies sometimes don't live, or a mom has a miscarriage. It was a beginning to understanding life.

One student referred to the classroom as an "animal farm." A teacher told me it surely was a "reproductive" room. Yes, on both counts, but it was filled with love for all living things.

While microscopic creatures may not be called "critters," they are living things. I usually brought in pond water during our study of the wetlands, and let the students use microscopes to see all the amazing little creatures. We had several gallon jars of water, filled with algae and some muck. We always found water fleas and little worms, and sometimes the larvae of mayflies. Leaches were great fun. The students would suck up the little ones in the droppers and put them on a slide and watch them stretch and move.

Probably the most exciting times were the years we found hydras in the water. One year we managed to find a hydra that had a baby branching off its side. Betty ran down the hallway, calling "Mr. T! Mr. T! (the principal) Come see! We have a pregnant hydra!" It was always difficult for an administrator, not knowing what was going on in our classroom.

And sometimes, those critters were not alive. One spring day we had a thunderstorm, and when I went out to check my rose buses, I spotted a dead bird. It was a sora rail. I had never seen one before, and wasn't even aware they lived around here. I put it in the freezer to take to school. And then, a few weeks later, we had another cold, windy spell and on the pavement in front of the garage door was a beautiful warbler, a tiny common yellowthroat. We had been listening to one on our nature trail, so I bagged him up and showed him to the students. Knowing it was illegal to keep dead song birds (or their feathers), I disposed of them as soon as the students had a chance to see them. One cold evening I found a tiny dead shrew outside my back door. What did I do? Of course, I put it in the freezer until I could take it in to share with the students. After all, how often do you see a shrew up close? One teacher told me that she wouldn't want to look in my freezer.

On Aquariums

When our new program was located in Corunna, Jayne, my teaching partner, suggested setting up an aquarium in our shared "enrichment" room.

I had had no previous experience with one, so I let her take charge. She put real plants in it, and it looked beautiful. Soon the water started turning yellow, and one of her goldfish died. The two I purchased seemed to be doing okay at the time. It wasn't long before algae took over. My son, Ed, told her that she had too much gravel. Since he had never worked with an aquarium before, I think she thought he was talking through his hat. The next day the assistant superintendent stopped in and said, "I think you have too much gravel."

That did it. She and Ed took it apart and reassembled it, using artificial plants. It looked cute with a new shipwreck bubbler in it. Then the brown algae took over. I bought two algae eaters, but the stuff had too much of a head start and one of them promptly died. We had some good moments, though. One of my students said he really liked to watch the "allergy" eaters.

We prepared to tear it down again, after one of Jayne's students brought in some algae destroying pills. Great! They even destroyed the last algae eater. Jayne decided to tear it down again, heat it, and put in tropical fish. We bought a swordtail, some angelfish, and a newt that called "Figgy."

After we moved to the Vernon building, I bought a plecastomus, which I called "Charles" because he resembled the puffed up, egotistical character on the TV show MASH. Charles was fun to watch, even though he didn't move much . . . or didn't until he decided to get rambunctious one day. One of the students went into the room to work one day and found him on the floor. How he had the energy to flip out was surprising. At least he was still alive, so I put him back and he survived.

I bought some new swordtails, and the day after I bought them we noticed some little things swimming around. They were little baby swordtails! I rushed out to get a plastic container that fits in the water to isolate the babies so they wouldn't get eaten. It was becoming an expensive project!

The aquarium became a pain to keep, because I had to come in on vacations to feed the fish, and it seemed like something was always going wrong. I finally took the remaining fish to the pet store—even my beloved Charles. I had learned a lot from having a fish tank—it taught me to avoid them.

After the fish, I brought in hermit crabs. Was this the right thing to have? They were fun to watch when they'd come out, but you rarely saw them when they were active. One student brought one of hers in and he was the friendliest little guy. He'd walk all over your hand and drink water from your palm.

The students couldn't handle our crabs, because they would pinch. When they died I called it quits on crabs.

Despite the trials and tribulations of pets in the classroom, I still believe they play an important role in the education process, and even today I stop to pet the hamsters, rabbits, guinea pigs and "show and tell" pets that I find in classrooms.

Play-ing Around with Drama

I have often maintained that teachers need to be actors. We need to pretend we're not sick when we are. We need to pretend we're not upset when we are. We need to show excitement about learning, because when we don't the students can read us. And we need to do crazy skits for the students to enjoy—for them to see that we are real people.

After one of the teacher skits on Young Author's Day my students wanted to know why some teachers (namely one) never had big roles. "Is it because they're not good actors?"

My answer could have been "Yes," because even in the classroom they might be boring. However, I told them that some teachers didn't really like acting. Someone said, "Mr. A is the singer of the building, not an actor." Good point, I thought.

Lauren asked, "Was Mrs. K the one who wasn't an actor?"

This particular teacher had NO sense of humor, and could never relax around the students. She was a drill sergeant who never smiled in the classroom. I answered, "She doesn't like funny roles," and didn't go into detail. Perceptive?

The first real experience I had with drama in the classroom was with the story of Hansel and Gretel, as told about in the section on "Reading." I was hooked with the students' interest and performance, so I decided to add more drama. I had the students make papier-mache puppets and write little plays for them. I had a puppet corner in the classroom, and it was rarely empty. The students created an elephant, a Snoopy dog, children and clowns. I was impressed with how much they loved to be making up little plays. I decided I had been missing a part of the "total child" in teaching.

For several years after that my students put on short plays at Christmas. Most scripts were from a play magazine, and included plays like *Randy the Red Horned Rainmoose,* and *The Year Santa Slept In.* They weren't creative story lines, but it gave the students a chance to be in front of an audience, wear a costume and "act" like someone (or something) else. Because of a lack of facilities and time, these holiday plays and classroom puppet shows formed my "drama curriculum" until I started teaching in the gifted and talented program.

Jayne, teacher of the fourth and fifth grade, was my mentor for drama through those years. She planned and directed plays that included the students from both my class and hers. Two of the early plays we did were "Alice in Wonderland" and "The Wizard of Oz." Parents, bless them, helped with extensive costuming and constructing props. When our class load was up to 40, Jayne asked to go it alone. That last year together she directed "Theater in the Round" with mythology.

One student exemplified what drama can do for a student's self image. Ellen, as a second grader, asked to be a tree. She could stand behind a prop, with only her face showing, and that would be painted to blend in with the trunk. She need not say a word. Every year she took a larger role, until when she was in Jayne's fifth grade, she performed a solo pantomime during the mythology presentations, and also presented a monologue. She was on stage by herself. Need I say more?

For the last several years of our program my students performed by themselves. Our plays were not the most professional, but the students loved every performance. We presented a melodrama, *"Billy Bart, the Scourge of the West,"* a Melodrama; *"The Golden Goose,"* a comedy, and using our own, original script we presented *"Dinosaur Park."*

I will never forget Bob, in "The Golden Goose." He was a regular clown, and played the part of simple-minded Dumling to a "T." But most memorable was when he graduated from high school. He sent me a note thanking me for attending his graduation open house. In the note he said "Thank you for letting me play Dumling." He never forgot that role. And Jenny wrote me years later about her being "tied" on the railroad tracks in "Billy Bart."

We studied African folktales, and performed several Anansi and Tall Tale Man skits. We brought art into the folktale studies by creating papier mache African masks, which decorated the stage.

Edward Lear and the *Just So Stories* were celebrated with *How the Camel Got His Hump* and *The Elephant's Child.*

Probably the largest play that my students performed was *"Constitution,"* a play to celebrate the 200th year of the United States Constitution. There were over 40 cast members, so I included students from the regular fourth and fifth grades. Parents were wonderful with making costumes, and I even sewed some "Ben Franklin" suits myself. In the play, "James Madison" was to sing George M. Cohan's "I'm a Yankee Doodle Dandy." Any volunteers? One fifth grader from another room said he "thought" he could do it. And sing he did. James had audience members in tears. It was the first time he had been heard, and even *he* didn't know he was so good.

As James went to high school, the drama bug stayed with him, and he joined the Owosso Players. He went on to play a starring role in "*Joseph and the Amazing Technicolor Dreamcoat*," where he sang a solo. I believe James realized what he could do when he sang that patriotic song.

While not such a "big" production, "*Dinosaur Park*" was indeed a favorite. We brainstormed a list of ideas to use. They included:

A time machine
A mad scientist
Dinosaurs brought to today's time
Trouble with today's food . . . they could get fat
Trouble with the ozone layer and the dinosaur's eyes
How to return the dinosaurs

The costumes were simple. We needed eight dinosaur suits. There were two professors, Professor Eon and Professor Time. We had Mother Nature, a dinosaur keeper, a dinosaur catcher, and gardeners and construction workers to get the park ready. Of course, some environmentalists were necessary, as were a reporter and photographer to get the news out. And how about a family to visit the park? We needed a dentist and an eye doctor. And then, to top it off, Mr. Bucks, the man who financed the whole project.

I was impressed with how quickly the kids learned their parts. They painted props and the time machine, which was, of course a refrigerator box. We presented it to the entire school, and the students laughed and clapped. However, the evening performance for the parents was disappointing. The acting was outstanding, but many in the audience did not understand the subtle humor, and were not responsive as the school students had been. I guess that's a part of the generation gap. I think the thing I was most proud of was that the play was created and presented before the movie, *Jurassic Park* was announced. We were ahead of the film industry, and proud of it.

We presented skits for Earth Day, which were sometimes our own creation and sometimes followed a pre-written script. One stands out because of the creativity it allowed. My fourth and fifth graders had been studying the environment, and divided into groups to present some way humans have negatively impacted the environment. Each group created its own skit, costumes, and props. An example of one performance was on water pollution. The students created a "boat" from a large piece of cardboard. They proceeded to throw their garbage into the "water," and the "fish" threw it back at them. The garbage included references to human wastes as well as food and food containers. One of the students brought a tape of a toilet flushing, and had made a toilet out of a box. They created original songs about picking up litter. This was done in a humorous fashion, but the students' message came across loud and strong.

The year that I visited the home of Laura Ingalls Wilder in Mansfield, Missouri with my niece and her friend, we also visited Hannibal, where we saw the replica fence that Tom Sawyer whitewashed in Mark Twain's famous book. We saw all the homes of the people in the story, and even went on a voyage down the Mississippi River on a paddlewheel steamer. We had taken the school's video camera, and I taped the steamer coming down the river, and when we were on it I placed the camera on a tripod, and taped the entire trip. Ideas came floating into my head. We would study river systems for social studies. Rivers were important in the growth of cities all over the world, and we would look at larger river systems as well as Shiawassee County.

We read *Tom Sawyer*, and some of Mark's Twains humorous short stories, like *Taming the Bicycle*, and *The Celebrated Jumping Frog of Calaveras County*. We made a skit out of the whitewashing scene from *Tom Sawyer* and videotaped it. The students created a time machine and Jim was a reporter who went back in time to interview Mark Twain and his wife.

We studied Lewis and Clark and their trip to the Pacific Ocean. Jim also interviewed the two explorers as well as Sacagawea. The most humorous part of this taping was when Sacagawea told about filling the baby carrier with sphagnum moss, to help absorb the baby's urine.

We looked at the local Shiawassee River, and read about the first white trader in the county, Whitmore Knaggs. Several students and I made a trip to the area near where his trading post had stood. We taped Mary telling about his life on the river and how a village grew near his trading post. Of course the village has been long gone, but there is still a cemetery where some of the counties earliest inhabitants are buried. The cemetery was also included in our story of the area. The students were interested in the fact that the men who founded the largest city in Shiawassee County came through the Knaggs area, and visited Whitmore Knaggs at his trading post. When a friend of mine who lived across from the cemetery saw an interest in the cemetery, he took it upon himself to see that the long neglected cemetery was cleaned up, and being a man whose hobby was woodworking, even made a nice sign for it.

We then took the videotapes to a local movie producer, who helped the students put all the scenes together into a movie on River Systems. We used the Mississippi River boat as an opening scene, and it was perfect. The students actually did the video work and I was impressed that they took to working the equipment quicker than I did. We set up several TVs in the gym, cabled them together, and shared the movie with the parents. While it wasn't actually a play, it was drama plus.

The study of Mark Twain fell during the perfect year of his 150th birthday. Of course, the students wanted a party. We ordered a huge birthday cake, dressed up our own Mark Twain and his wife, and shared the birthday cake with the entire school for a dessert at lunch. Mark and his wife cut the cake and served it.

You can tell that the actual acting was just one part of the performances. The plays were usually an offshoot of our curriculum . . . the environment, fairy tales, folk tales, history, etc. They included music, the creation of props, and most importantly, working together. Practices were usually done in the classroom, and the students' desks often competed with the construction of props. It is the teacher who must decide what is important. If the drama coincides with the curriculum, it can be fit in. And each teacher must decide if students will retain more from reading a book or hearing a lecture . . . or from researching, and then writing and presenting a script.

The Good, The Oops!
and the Funny

Many memorable things happen during the course of a teaching career. Some you are proud of, some are not so good except for the lessons you learn, and some are just funny. In this chapter I will try to relate some of these in hopes the reader might learn from them or just have a chuckle or two.

In the Bloomingdale Public Schools the classroom was certainly diverse. There were middle-class whites and blacks, as well as children of migrant workers. There were also some very poor whites. In my fourth grade one girl was 13—three years older than the rest. Physically she appeared to be around 10, so the age difference wasn't obvious to the other students. She also was very low functioning academically—and socially, she just didn't seem to fit. Emma felt comfortable talking to me, and I enjoyed listening to her. One day she told me that she had never had a baby doll. I talked to our faithful minister's wife, and the next day Emma had her doll. She was thrilled.

I was working on a bulletin board one day during recess and she asked me, "Mrs. Labadie, when you start bleeding, what does that mean?" I gulped and thoughts ran through my head—does she understand the facts of life? Do I dare tell her if she doesn't? I managed to say, "Why do you need to know?" She responded with, "My goat is expecting triplets, and this morning she started bleeding. Does that mean she might have the babies soon?"

"Whew!" To myself I breathed a sigh of relief. To her, I told her that the goat probably would have the babies soon. The next day she announced that the goat did indeed have her triplets, and she asked me if I would come see them. I told her that I would give them a couple of weeks, and then I would be happy to visit.

House visits can be risky, and I wasn't sure what to expect. I had never met her parents, and Emma wasn't always the cleanest in appearance, so I was a little hesitant. However, I had promised. I gathered up my 3-year-old son, and instructed him that no matter what the house was like, he wasn't supposed to say anything that would hurt the family's feelings. We were just going to see the goats.

Her parents were older than I thought they'd be, were pleasant, and clean in appearance. Two older brothers were working on cars, and looked like they hadn't cleaned the grease off in days. One of the brothers had a new baby in the house, but I didn't think I'd go in. The windows were crammed full of "stuff." However, the baby goats were darling and my son loved them. He chased a pair of geese around, looked at the many dogs, cats and chickens, and was very polite. When we pulled out of the driveway, he said, "Boy, that was sure a messy place." And I said, "Bless you, my son." But the best thing was that it pleased Emma that I thought enough of her to visit.

Storm

In January 1979 I had a frightening experience—possibly one of the most frightening in all my years. I was teaching in the old Shiawassee Street building, which once had housed the entire school district. It was the second year of our gifted and talented program, and there were only our two classrooms—mine and the fourth and fifth grade. The administrative offices were across the large hallway. The first floor was almost like a second floor, with steps going down to the basement and up to our rooms. My room was large and had high ceilings. The west walls were full of tall windows, and next to the windows was a door that opened to steps leading down to the playground. Above the door was a large glass transom.

The winter had been warm—40 + degrees many days. There wasn't much snow, and only a little rain. One wet, windy day, I sent the children to the Elsa Meyer building for their lunch, and sat at my desk while I devoured a thermos of chili. I had been working at the back of the room near the door and windows, helping the students and checking papers.

After eating I stood up to go back to the table to complete my work, and had second thoughts. I decided to finish my lesson plans at my desk. About five minutes later the outdoors turned dark and a big gust of wind hit the windows. As I looked up, the large window above the back door blew in—and the wind howled throughout the room. There was an eerie feeling and I almost hesitated, wondering what to do. I fought through the wind to the hallway door and was about to lie on the floor (as in a tornado) when our community education director came into the hall to see what was going on. I was visibly shaken but unhurt.

We went back into the classroom to survey the damage. The wind had died down quickly and the sky was lighter. The table where I had been working before the children left was covered with glass. I picked up some papers and put a gash in my finger that later required a stitch to close. The papers on the table were not blown around, but were soaked. Construction paper that had been on a shelf was blown around the room, however. There was a one-fourth inch gap between the ceiling and the partition that divided my room from Jayne's, and sawdust blew through that gap and covered the desks in her room. How thankful I was that the children were not there, and that I had stayed at my desk to work.

Teacher Dress

When it came to clothing appropriate for teaching, in the early '60s women always wore skirts. Slacks were rarely worn at home and never at school. Pantyhose wasn't common then, so we had to wear a girdle or a garter belt to hold up our nylon stockings. One day I was giving a spelling test and walking around the room while reciting the words. I felt one of the fasteners let go. As if that wasn't bad enough, the other one on the same leg came undone and the nylon started slipping down my leg. I walked slowly, so as not to attract attention, toward the door, but by the time I reached the doorway, the stocking was around my ankle. There was a bathroom in the hallway just outside our door, so I went in and reattached the nylon. The students wondered why I left, but I thought it best left unsaid.

What color shoes do you wear? One year I had a new pair of comfortable shoes that were a butterscotch color. One of my boys noticed. He said, "You have new shoes." "Yes," I said. "Do you like them?" He paused a moment, and answered, "Well, black goes with everything." Guess that was my answer.

Recess duty during the winter was tough when you had to wear a skirt. When snowmobiles became popular, I bought a green John Deere snowmobile suit. It was so easy to step into it, even with a skirt on. The students called me the "Jolly Green Giant," and I *was* jolly because I kept warm while the other teachers stood outside freezing. I played fox and geese and made snow forts with the students. As the years progressed I matured a little and purchased a long down coat. I kept warm, but couldn't play in the snow as much.

When pantsuits came into style, I hurried out and bought one. Such comfort! And, from Dan's observation, much more practical. Dan was in my son's second grade classroom. Not long after school started I asked him how he liked his teacher. "Just fine," he reported. "Especially when she bends over." Needless to say, students notice. Short skirts are not for teaching.

Another fashion trend that came about more recently is low slung pants and tops that stop above the pants. In other words, one bends over and the students see your "crack," or you raise your hand and your midriff shows. I have heard of a young teacher bending over and showing off her "thong" underwear. We need to be more conservative, gang.

Difficult Students and a Scare

During my second year in Vernon, I noticed that a second grader spent a lot of time in the hallway. His teacher was "older," and had no patience. The student would get mad, and then the teacher would yell. The student would yell back, so he was sent into the hallway. How glorious for him. He was thrilled because he didn't have to do any work.

When I received Dale into my classroom, I was careful not to become impatient. He was behind academically, and the school received no support from the family. When MEAP tests first started, these parents told their sons to leave and come home instead of taking the tests. When I had Dale's fall conference, his mother told me the reason he was behind was all the "rotten" teachers he had had. Well, I had questioned his second grade teacher, but where did the initial problems lie?

One day when I was going over work with another child, Dale came up and insisted on getting my attention. I admit I was a little exasperated, and told him to wait until I was finished. He stamped back to his desk and slammed his head down. I immediately saw that I was wrong. Even though I hadn't raised my voice, he took it as rejection. I was more careful in how I talked to him after that. And you know, it worked. I was able to acquire an aide to help him with his work, and with both of us being firm but gentle, he progressed. Slowly, but he progressed. And I progressed. I always remembered that gentleness could help even when things aren't going right.

That year I was lucky enough to have a student teacher for the second semester. The students loved Max, and we worked well together. However, things suddenly went downhill with Dale. He didn't want to go out for recess, and stayed close by me. He started throwing his books and coat on the floor, and stuffed everything else into his desk. During lessons he'd put his head down on his desk. After discussions with Max, the principal, my aide, and the special reading teacher, we came to the conclusion that he was afraid he would lose me. The introduction of Max into the classroom was a difficult adjustment for him. He finally came to see that I wasn't leaving, and Max started working more one on one with him instead of letting him retreat into a shell. It worked. He was his own perky, lovable self again. I didn't have control over the happenings the following years, and Dale eventually dropped out of school. Of course I felt frustrated, but unfortunately, we teachers are only one player in the life of a child. We tend to feel we can change every child's life, but that just doesn't happen. We can only do the best for every child when we have them in our classrooms. We need to love them when we can.

There were few things scarier than not knowing where a child was. One day Andrew went to the bathroom at 1:30, and didn't return. I talked to the principal, and he called Andrew's mother, to see if he had walked the few blocks to his home. He hadn't. She drove around town looking for him, with no luck. School dismissed at 2:30, so by the time she returned home, school was out. Before she could call the police, Andrew walked in the front door of his house as if nothing had happened. He admitted he had hidden at a neighbor's until school was out. Of course, we had long talks with him and his mother grounded him, but I don't think he really understood. I prayed for some way to help this boy, who was calling out for it. I referred him for a possible new "resource room," and he qualified, but the room didn't materialize for several years. Andrew became a dropout.

School Trips

In some years we took after-school bus trips to a roller skating rink. Even though I wasn't a great skater, I joined in the fun. On one of the trips, Kay, our special reading teacher, joined us. She skated gracefully and certainly outshone me. One of the special "skates" was when everyone had to skate backward. That left me out, but Kay moved beautifully down the length of the rink backwards, until she hit the brick wall. She apparently misjudged the distance, and upon hitting the wall, slid to a sitting position on the floor. Oops! Her wig didn't slide down with her, but stuck to the bricks where she had hit. She reached up, grabbed the wig and plopped it on her head. Not all the staff saw it, but the few of us who did laughed heartily. Kay skated over to us, and laughingly said, "You'd better not put that in the school paper!" After that comment I laughed so hard I slipped and fell to the floor, pulling Kay down with me. My stomach hurt so badly I had a difficult time getting up. Some of the students wondered what we saw as so funny. Thankfully, only a few saw her fall.

The next day my students asked me if I fell much. I answered that I didn't fall while skating. Ken offered, "Yeah, but Mrs. M did when her wig fell off." Everyone just looked at him quizzically, as if to say, "What wig?" I quickly changed the subject and the matter was forgotten—but I wondered how many students went home and told their parents that Mrs. M wore a wig.

Another adventure was a trip to Arkona, Canada. I invited all my kids and their parents to meet me at Rock Glen, in Arkona on a Saturday just after school was out in June, where I would take them on a fossil hunt I took one student, the Black family arrived in their motor home, Tom and his mother were there, Jason and his family, and Alice and her father. We toured the little museum so the students could see what they "might" find, and went out to the stream where we waded, looking for brachiopods. Some of us had knee boots and others wore old tennis shoes that could be discarded afterwards. I don't know who enjoyed it more—the kids, the parents, or me. While we were in the shallows, a group of ladies came wading through the center of stream, where it was knee deep. They were screeching about being afraid. I told them it was okay, except for the leeches. More screeching! I qualified it by saying leeches were generally in the quieter areas. They felt better then and quieted down, but I chuckled to myself and to my group, because we knew they were all over. After lunch we drove to an area near a river, where we climbed the exposed slopes and gathered more "treasures." Everyone went home with bags of fossils, and the students really felt like paleontologists. An ideal trip that I wish all of my students could have experienced.

Assisting on Far Away Trips

Jayne was more adventurous when it came to taking long distance trips, but she was kind enough to let me go along to help when it was needed. Her students were participating in Odyssey of the Mind, a competition of creative presentations and spontaneous, creative mental responses. Every year at least one of her teams would make it to the state level in competition, and one team even made it to the world finals. How lucky we were that it was to be held in Flagstaff, Arizona! Jayne received tremendous support from the school board and community, and plans were made for the students on the winning team to fly to Phoenix. They would then take a bus to Flagstaff. Many parents accompanied the team, and I was lucky enough to go along to be "chief videographer," and since the competition was a first for our district, the principal even took time off to go.

The plane trip was exciting for the students. I must say that the other passengers were very tolerant, because the students went from window to window to see the mountains and rivers. It was a fantastic geography lesson. The students responded with applause when the plane landed, and excitedly boarded a bus for Flagstaff.

I sat next to Tim, the six-year-old brother of one of the students. What fun it was to observe the western panorama through his eyes. The saguaro cactus, sagebrush and tumbleweeds brought to my mind the cowboy shows of my youth. I fully expected to see Hopalong Cassidy or the Lone Ranger riding alongside the bus.

Our school had purchased a video camera for us, but to get a really good one that was of commercial quality, it had a separate power pack. So, everywhere we went I had the power pack on one arm, my personal tote on the other, and the camera held by both hands. Good thing I was balanced. We hiked down into Oak Creek Canyon, and walked the trails of the cliff dwelling Native Americans. We wandered around Sunset Crater stood on old lava flows, and traipsed through an ancient pueblo. History came alive for all. .

Probably the most memorable adventure was visiting the Grand Canyon. We started out on a tram, which stopped at various locations so we could get out and look at the vistas. After a few stops, I felt like I was missing something. I wasn't the only one of our group who felt that way, so a few families and I left the tram and hiked the rim. No railings, of course, and with an active six year old! Good thing his dad was there to guide him. We went down into the canyon on Bright Angel Trail, as far as we thought we could go in the allotted time. I'm so glad I read the book *"Brighty of the Grand Canyon"* to the students because legend has it that he created the trail. Seeing the beauty of the canyons through the eyes of the students was certainly a highlight. After our return to Corunna I told the superintendent that I would like to make a request—that when my class studies geography, we take a plane trip to the west so the students can see first hand the mountains, deserts and river systems. Why wouldn't he listen?

Despite the loss of the props for the students' production, the team did well, and we flew home with smiles. My mother met the plane in Flint with balloons for the students, and all went to their respective homes with unforgettable memories.

Another trip that I accompanied Jayne on was not so far away. Her students had pen pals in Canada, and she wanted to take the class to their school and visit Toronto. I went along to help monitor, since her entire class was going, and of course some parents. There were almost 30 of us as we boarded the school bus for Sarnia, where we'd catch the train to where we'd meet the students. We spent that night at the school with the pen pals—sleeping on the floor of the library. Now, I am adventurous, but a sleeping bag on a school floor was not really my idea of an adventure—but for Jayne and the students, I managed. Not a restful night, but I did it.

We then took a train into Toronto, and needed to get onto the subway. Try to get all of us on quickly! We pushed the kids on so no one would be missed, but Jayne's aide almost got stuck in the closing door. Jayne is sophisticated in the ways of the world, and had a bright umbrella. She stood by the door and waved it so the conductor could see it. He opened the door again. Whew! We were off. And then, we had to push the kids off the subway so we'd all be together.

Going down sidewalks Jayne held her umbrella high so we all could see it in the crowds of people. I felt like we were in a parade, and I guess we were. We headed for our last stops, dinner at the Spaghetti Factory, a trip to the CN Tower and a hostel for the night. Sleeping in European sheets was a trip in itself. The sheet is like a sleeping bag, and you feel like a pupa inside a cocoon. It was a good thing I didn't have to get up during the night, because I would probably have ended up on the floor.

I must reflect on the question—how many of us would even think of taking twenty plus students on a trip across the border, on a train and subway . . . and sleeping in a hostel. I would never have made the trip except for Jayne's enthusiasm and organization. And I sure appreciated her inviting me. I must also admit, that on the two major trips I went with her, there was not a single act of misbehavior by the students. Hopefully, it will encourage others to not be afraid to attempt such adventures.

A Memorable Museum Trip

I often took my students to the Exhibit Museum at the University of Michigan. We usually went on a Saturday, because the crowd was thinner and you didn't have to worry about other noisy school groups. Parents were always eager to go, and we would have one or two parents to four or five students.

There were dinosaurs on display, a mastodon that was found not far from our town in the 1940s, an abundance of fossils, and many mounted present day animals from Michigan. The museum isn't huge, so the students didn't get tired or bored.

In 1991 I joined a fossil group that supported the museum, and was able to go on fossil hunting trips and help with field work as well as assist as a volunteer in the labs or wherever help was needed. This gave me even more insight into the workings of the museum, as well as first hand knowledge of some of the displays.

After I became principal, I was asked to go on a trip with a second grade group during the week. I talked to the students about what they would see, and served as a guide for the displays. In one area an edmontosaurus lies on what appears to be sand, to represent how he was found. One of the students looked at me and said, "Mrs. Labadie, did he look like that when you found him?" Another student, when looking at dioramas that had a mounted sandhill crane with eggs and newly hatched chicks, someone asked, "Are there dinosaurs in the eggs?"

Probably the most memorable trip can be related in the following story.

What if it's the Ku Klux Klan?

The large yellow bus came to a stop on the busy city street. There were black and yellow barricades and detour signs that directed traffic to the north. "Only two more blocks and we would have been on Main Street!" I moaned to myself. Why are they detouring traffic? Then, a mass of bodies appeared, walking on the street, coming directly at us. While looking at the traffic and the traffic light situation, I was trying to explain to the driver what she would need to do to get out of town and onto U.S. 23 north. One of the students exclaimed, "They're wearing masks!" Another replied, "Maybe it's the Ku Klux Klan!" As the light changed and the bus turned north onto Fourth Ave., I glanced in the direction of the marchers. They also were turning north, into the grounds of the county office complex. I turned to the back of the bus and the students who had been talking. "No, not the Ku Klux Klan," I reassured them. The marchers out of our sight now, we concentrated on getting the bus around construction barrels and out of town. I took the loudspeaker again and said, "Someone should watch the news tonight to see what's going on."

"Yes," someone added, "If you see a yellow bus, that's us!"

Once safely on 23, we settled down for a nice return trip home. The students asked for the radio to be turned on, and we had a nice ride home with the skylights open and the radio turned up to a volume that only kids enjoy. I had to move out of the seat I was in because it was directly under a speaker, and my ears can only tolerate so many decibels.

The driver decided that since we took a different route out of Ann Arbor, we'd take a different way home. We came up 23 and turned west on Thompson Road, to eventually come through the town of Durand. I shared with them the view of the railroad depot and the bronze statue created by my friend, a local artist. I showed them where the nature trail built by my students had been—and where in the past several years we have sighted an eagle. As the kids sang their way home, I thought about how great a trip we had had.

The students had been eager to visit the University of Michigan Ruthven Museum of Natural History in Ann Arbor. We had left school at 8:25 and had driven down 23 and were almost to Ann Arbor, when I had the driver go to the east on M-14 so the kids could see the sights. I said, "This is your tour guide," and all laughed. I pointed out Domino's Farms, and we marveled at the size of the massive buildings. I pointed out the Geddes Road exit, where their teacher had gone to college at Concordia. She showed the dorms and soccer field, which could be seen from the highway.

Then there was Hogback Road. The students had studied glaciers in class, so I was sure to point out the road as a glacier "leftover." We turned off the expressway onto Washtenaw Avenue, and I pointed the way to Eastern Michigan University, my Alma Mater. As we turned to go onto the campus of the University of Michigan we enjoyed the view of the beautiful and historic looking sorority and fraternity homes.

The museum was our destination. The students first viewed the planetarium show, while I went to see if the paleontologist was in. (He wasn't.) Then the students, in small groups, toured the museum, with me giving mini-lectures on some of the displays, especially in the Hall of Evolution. I enjoyed sharing my experiences helping to recover mastodon bones and in the preservation of mastodon footprints that were in a "trackway" on display. The students and parents alike were eager and responsive. I was proud of their knowledge and curiosity, and proud of their conduct. While waiting for the groups to finish and return to the lobby, the director of the planetarium joined us. I introduced him to several of our small groups as they came by. A couple of months previous to this, the director had brought an outreach program on space to the Corunna fifth graders. I had known him for about 10 years, through fossil hunting and space programs through the museum. Devon immediately looked at him, and said, "I saw you!" The director laughed, and responded, "And I remember you!" How could he forget Devon?

When several groups had gathered I took them outside to wait, since the weather was sunny and warm. We watched two helicopters circling the area. One of them, we managed to see, had FOX on it. I thought out loud, "Fox is a TV network." We all laughed. The planes had been circling since the groups had gone to lunch. The kids waved at the copters, and someone said, "Maybe there's a riot, like there was at Michigan State last week!" We laughed again as we went to the bus, and later encountered the detours and the marchers on Huron Street.

After I arrived home, I called my sister, who lived in Ypsilanti, a short distance from Ann Arbor. "What was going on in Ann Arbor today?"

Her reply? "A Ku Klux Klan rally!"

"Oh, brother," I countered. "And we were almost in the middle of it. Wait until the Superintendent hears this! What if we're on TV, driving in a Ku Klux Klan rally!"

Note: On the 10:00 news it was reported that after the marchers reached the county complex, the rally turned violent and tear gas was used. This had to be right after we saw them. I must admit, it was scary watching the people advance toward us, with us not knowing what was happening.

Word Mix-ups

When my son was in fifth grade, the teacher received word that a former student would be returning. The previous year he had been placed in a different building so he could have use of a resource room, but was "tested out" of the special education program. He was to go into my son's classroom. At dinner one night I said to him, "I hear you will be getting a new student."

"Yeah," he said, "and when he was in our room last year it was a regular whore house."

"A what?" I quickly asked.

"A whore house!"

"A what?" I couldn't believe my ears! Then, after he repeated it again, and I asked "A what?" for the third time, he came back with "Well, when he was in our room last year his desk was like a house of horror!"

"Whew!" I took a deep breath and said, "Oh. I understand."

I had fun teasing the former teacher about the kind of a classroom she had.

The pronunciation of words can indeed be confusing. We were having a discussion on how our lives would be different if we didn't have airplanes (cars, etc.) "What words would be omitted from our vocabulary?" I asked.

"Well," said David. "How about hot pilots?" When I asked him what he meant, he said, "You know, cold pilots and hot pilots to fly the planes."

I thought a minute and then it dawned on me. I wrote, "co-pilot" on the board and explained his role on a plane. Apparently David thought that the "co" was "cold." And if there was a cold pilot, why wasn't there a hot pilot?

Denise came up to me and asked me how to spell "piddow." It took me a second or two to think, and asked her what she meant. "You sleep on it," was her answer. She had always called a pillow a piddow. Children don't always hear clearly what we are saying, and sometimes we're afraid to correct them.

And then there was the time we were talking about homonyms. The students were calling them out and I would write them on the board. "Do, due and dew," someone suggested. Another student interjected, "And then there's doo-doo!"

Here's a couple of other definitions;

krill—something you barbeque on
blubber—belly flops

When I told the students that we would be working with synonyms, Carson blurted out, "Oh, goody! Something to eat!"

While this is not about words, it is certainly about misunderstanding something. Sixth graders had not been in our building for many years. The school system had clustered them in one building so the teachers could departmentalize the curricular areas. At one point they were returned to the individual buildings while a new high school was being built. The old high school would be converted into a middle school and the sixth grade would be attending there when all construction was completed. In order to accommodate the sixth grade girls and their sanitary needs, a napkin dispenser was put in the girls' restroom. One first grader brought a sanitary napkin into the office, and told the secretary that she wanted her money back. She saw that it was a place to put a nickel, and thought maybe she would get candy or gum. I have an addendum to this. The schools soon removed the dispensers and kept the newer, self-adhesive napkins in the health room for the girls.

During a reading lesson the word "thud" came up. When a second grader asked about it, Ricky said, "Dishes were washed with soap thuds." Teachers really need to be good at deciphering words.

"And some students know big words but don't realize they use them incorrectly. My son's second grade teacher told me that one day several students were having a disagreement. She told them they shouldn't be feuding. Someone asked what feuding meant, so she asked if anyone knew. Leave it to Ed—he raised his hand and said, "Well, it's like when you need to go to the bathroom but you don't go." The teacher didn't really understand what he meant, until she thought about it. I told her that his answer was a polite way to say, "farting." She agreed.

How Old Are You, Teacher?

When you do your student teaching (or internship), it's not unusual for students to fall in love with you. Such was the case in 1962 with Raymond and Danny. Danny wanted to be older so he could marry me, and Raymond was the little guy with the huge vocabulary.

Years later—in fact, it was in the late 1980s—my mother was working on an election board for Ypsilanti Township, when a lady asked her, "Aren't you Sally's mother? The one who student taught at Begole School?" When my mother said yes, she said, "Well, I'm Raymond's mother, and he still loves her." That was over 20 years later! What a compliment.

When we lived in Bloomingdale my husband's boss told me a story that was related to him by a good friend who was the father of one of my students. It seems this student was eating dinner with his family, and was talking about school and probably specifically about something I was doing with the students. (Maybe running through the woods with them?) The father asked, "Just how old is this Mrs. Labadie anyway?"

The son replied, "I don't know, but she's getting up there."

Getting up there? I was only 25 years old!

A few years later I was on a Saturday bus trip with a group of sixth grade safety patrols. Jennifer, once one of my third graders, was trying to find out my age. I just laughed and said, "19"

Jennifer came back, "Oh, Mrs. Labadie-I'll bet you're—oh, about 22?" I said nothing, just smiled. Sharon said, "No, she's 26!" "Oh, come now," retorted Jennifer. "She's not an old hag!"

There was no way I was going to tell them I was over 30!

One Halloween I dressed up as George Washington, wearing a suit I had made my son for the bicentennial that same year. Yes, he was 12, but it fit me! Brian came up to me and very seriously said "I didn't know they made costumes that big!"

Our building always started the year off with a big potluck dinner, where the parents could meet all the teachers. I sat at a table with one of my students, Tom, and another teacher, Diane, and her husband. In a discussion about age, it came out that Diane was in her late 20s. When Tom found out I was 39, he came out with the "You sure don't look 39!" Which was a compliment, but he made it sound like 39 was as old as 80.

My birthday is in late August, so throughout my life I always missed celebrating it at school. Until, that is, we started opening school before Labor Day. When I was principal, Martha had her fifth graders make me birthday cards. Jack, who was smart, active, and all-boy, and who had spent some time in my office talking over problems, created one that I will always remember. It said,

> "Happy Birthday, Mrs. Labadie. Even know (though) you are principal, deep down inside I know you're a really nice person. Thanks for being my principal. What would I do with out you when I get in trouble? Hopefully I won't. This is our last year so let's make the best of it."

I'm glad he thought I was nice, even deep down inside. And **I'd** make the best of it, but would he? The card even had a drawing of a detention list. I wonder why! You must know, however, that I couldn't help but love that boy. He was a good student academically, and he had spunk!

One day I wore a necklace given to me by a student the previous year. One of my students commented on how much she liked it. I thanked her, and told her that Linda's (the giver's sister was in this class) sister had given it to me the year before. Charles said, "Boy, you sure keep things a long time!" Comes with age, my boy!

I was talking to my students about the music teacher and how she was going to retire. She had stated that she wanted to quit before she became a "grumpy old teacher." I said that I hoped to do that, too. Rhonda commented, "Well, you sure blew it!" We all laughed, and I told her, "Too bad, isn't it?"

Someone asked the age-old question (again) of how old I was. I didn't answer, and Connie offered, "52!" Someone said, "You sure don't look like 52!" (I was 37) Dear Lenny smiled his sweet smile and said, "That's because she uses Oil of Olay!" I didn't use it then, but do now!

Most days I would eat my lunch in the classroom and the students were free to stay in and work. However, there were times that I enjoyed a walk down the quiet streets of Vernon in the middle of the day. One day Jon asked if he could stay in to work on the computer. On that particular day, I told him, "No, I'm going for a walk during lunch."

He quipped, "At your age?" I replied with a grin, "Thanks, Jon—I'll remember to take my cane."

While the next story doesn't have to do with MY age, it bears repeating at this time. Rachel overheard Nancy and me talking about our taste buds after an article that she read stated, "older people lose some of their taste buds and that the ones left don't work well."

Rachel commented, "That's why my dad likes liver!" Her dad was "old." About 30.

One year our aide was hospitalized with a back injury. As the students made cards for her, they talked about her earlier announcement that she would be retiring. Someone asked, "How old do you have to be to retire?" Another student answered, "About 30." I cringed. I had missed five years of retirement pay!

Even college students have what to me is a distorted sense about age. In one of my administrative certification classes we were having a discussion analyzing an article on spelling lessons in the classroom that had been written in 1978. You must realize that I was the senior member of this class (50) . . . and everyone else was between the ages of 24 and 35. After talking about the article, one of the students said, "They sure were enlightened back then." I turned in my seat to see who said it, and thought, "Yes, back in the stone age." I should have stood and said, "Honey, wait until I get my cane so I can hit you with it."

While this doesn't have to do with age, it is about size. Tara's second graders were using meter sticks in the classroom, measuring everything, when Tara thought she heard someone behind her. She was busy, and glanced around, but paid no great heed to it. Suddenly a little girl said, "Mrs. H, you are 4 meters wide." She was measuring Tara's backside. It was bad enough to measure that area of Tara's body, but she also was measuring incorrectly.

Presidents

What do the students think when they see a real live president at school? One February we had a man who portrayed Abraham Lincoln come to talk to the fourth and fifth graders. He was tall and had dark hair. His make-up and costume made him look the part. As I was walking him to the library where the talk would take place, the first graders were heading out for recess and saw us in the hall. One of the little girls asked Pam, her teacher, if "Abe Lincoln was dead." Pam told her that he was. "Well," the girl added, in a confident voice, "then that must have been George Washington!" I ask you, how often do we talk about George Washington dying? At least she knew the presenter was a president.

My normal daily routine took me to the lunchroom to make sure all was going smoothly. As I talked to the students in the hot lunch line, Carson said, "Mrs. Labadie, the president was just here."

I asked, "The President?"

"Yes. You know, the man with the silver hair." At that time Bill Clinton was in office, and he had what appeared to be silver hair.

I asked Carson where the "president" had gone, and he told me that he went out of the lunchroom and down the hall. I asked him to wait a minute—that I'd be right back. I went into the hall, but no one was in the immediate vicinity. I looked around the corner and down the main hallway, and Matt, our fifth grade teacher, was heading for his classroom.

I returned to the lunchroom and asked Carson, "Was he wearing a suit?"

"No. He was wearing a green shirt with a dark blue collar."

"Could it have been Mr. McCall?"

"I guess maybe," he answered slowly.

Matt got a kick out of it. I'll always remember him as "Pres" or "Chief." After all, how many principals have a real live president in their building?

Intuition

Over the years I had always brought in a television to watch the many Saturn V rockets take off and land with our heroes, the astronauts. When the space shuttle started, I kept the same tradition. Space flight was still exciting to me, and I hated to see it become such a commonplace thing that people ignored it. I don't know why I changed my habit for the January, 1986 lift off of the Challenger space shuttle. I contemplated it, but decided against it for the first time. I had bad feelings about the flight, of which the first teacher was taking part.

And so, while we were working in the classroom our principal brought the news as soon as it was broadcast. The Challenger exploded on lift-off. Of course, we were all stunned. It was difficult to tell the kids, and they too, were shocked. However, like children, they wanted to talk about it. And talk we did.

When Death Intervenes

When you work with such active, bright little children you don't think of such things as losing a child. But it happens. The following are just a few of the precious children I taught who have left this earth.

Alex was a sweet towhead, but like most 9 year olds, he could be a "peeler," too. He had had trouble with reading, but with a lot of work was progressing. He was from a large family, and his mom and stepdad struggled financially. When Alex joined the Cub Scouts, I gave him my son's outgrown scout shirt, and he was proud to wear it. When he left for school in the morning, he was clean, but when he arrived at school he usually had dirt smudges. He loved the dirt and loved to play in it.

On the last day of school he hung around after the other children left, and wanted to talk. After some conversation, I had to things to do in the classroom, so I said, "You must be glad school is out." His answer was, "No, I like school." That was a sign of success. We said our goodbyes and I gave him a hug.

On July 31 I received a phone call and was asked whether Alex was the boy who just drowned at the Shiatown Dam. I frantically called our school secretary and neighbor to the family. She hadn't heard, but was going to check on it. Her return call? Yes. Alex had gone to the dam with an older boy, without his family knowing it. The older boy pushed Alex over the side of the river at the base of the dam "just for fun." Alex was pulled under the concrete skirt of the dam by the strong undertow.

I went to the funeral home, and I will never forget how clean Alex looked in his little white shirt. He was an angel. He was buried in a cemetery that is near the river, and his grandparents put a small marker there. I still occasionally stop by, and still shed tears.

This loss affected me so much that when I was a principal I told my teachers every year to "love the kids, because you don't know what will happen to them or where they will be. Love them while you have them."

I have had three former students take their own lives when they were in their 20s. It is so sad, and I always wonder if I could have done anything more to help them be more secure in life. Realistically—probably not, but the lingering thought is there. In addition, an automobile accident took the life of James, and being thrown off a horse caused the death of Marty. These boys were all so promising, happy and carefree as youngsters. They will always remain that way in my mind and heart.

When I became principal, I learned that Karla had cancer. Karla had been one of my third graders many years before, and she had written to me for several summers after that. When she had her only son she was in her 30s, and I took a crocheted afghan to the hospital. I saw her in a store parking lot two years later with her son, Terry. She told me I couldn't retire until I taught him.

However, although I didn't retire, I left the classroom, and Terry was one of my students when I was a principal. It was then I found out about Karla's illness. She struggled through cancer, and died when Terry was in second grade. Karla had told me that Terry had carried the afghan around until it fell apart, so after her death I created a small "memory" afghan that looked just like the original, and gave it to Terry.

Monica was in my third grade classroom the same year as Karla. Although I knew her older sister, I hadn't seen Monica since she left our building. When I became a principal, she called me about getting her daughter into my building for kindergarten. I was pleased to hear from her and tickled that she thought enough of me to move her daughter so I would work with her, but because of the bus routes and a full kindergarten load, my hands were tied. She called several times, but it just wouldn't work. It was after Karla's death that Monica was up north, and died when she hit a tree while snowmobiling. What a tragedy! She had been a bubbly, bright student, and was a concerned, caring mother, who was active in the building where her daughter attended.

And then there was Brad. Brad came to live with his father and stepmother, and was here for only a short time. He was quiet and withdrawn, so I moved him to the front of the classroom. It wasn't long before he started volunteering and answering questions. His parents took him to the mental health clinic, and they said he was fine, to just keep him busy and active. And that was okay with me, as our room was always buzzing with activity.

He moved back with his mother before the year was up, and I lost touch with his progress. I later had his stepbrother in class, but after he grew up I had no real connection to Brad, until one day, years later, when his stepmother came for a visit. She told me that Brad had died, overcome by gas, when working in a pit that brought utilities into his house trailer. I was crushed.

His stepmother told me that Brad was a caretaker at a wildlife refuge, and that "I didn't know how much I had influenced him." He came to love reading and nature. She gave the school a painting that she had done in his memory, and presented me with a decoupaged "book" that was open to a page with beautiful birds and flowers on one side, and the following verse on the other . . .

> I Love You . . .
> For seeing
> me as I wish I were,
> for hearing
> what I mean and not
> just what I say,
> for knowing
> how I feel,
> for helping
> me to grow.
>
> Judith Bond, 1986

The verse is one that is important for all teachers. It's one that parents and children think but don't say to us. Brad's name is engraved on the base, and it sits in my china cabinet so I can remember how important we are to the children.

There was also Michael, a quiet, thoughtful boy, with a quick wit and a good sense of humor. Michael played The Tall Tale Man in our production of *African Folktales.* When he was in the armed forces, he suddenly became ill and died of a rare congenital condition.

Larry died accidentally in Chicago. He had been working as a model, and dreamed of hitting the big stage. He was a beautiful human being, working on his goal in life—with that life suddenly cut short.

Jeff was a third grader in my room when, one evening, his house caught fire. His mother had run upstairs to get the older children, and their three year-old followed her without the mother knowing it. The older children jumped out the window, but the little girl died in the fire. The entire town and school community came together to support the family, but there was little we could do to ease their grief except to be there for them.

As a principal, I was shocked one day when the parent of a fifth grader came into my office and told me that her ex-husband, the child's father, had just been killed in an automobile accident. She was there to tell her son, and take him home. I found the social worker, and went to the classroom to get the boy. We all gathered in the social worker's room, and the mother told her son about the accident. He took it surprisingly well, and asked if he could let the class know. We all went to the classroom, where he told his classmates. Several students came and hugged him, and we adults did the same. I believe his letting the other students know was important in the initial stages of the grieving process.

I have sorrowed with the families at the loss of their children, as well as remembering with them the many successes in their child's short life. I have hugged children who have lost their parents, and talked with those who had parents who were struggling with tragic illnesses. We teachers have a tendency to wrap our hearts around the students, so we feel for them the rest of our lives. They are always with us.

Oh, That Messy Desk!

We all know that students do not enter school with great organizational skills. We must teach them those important skills. I always gave my students time to clean their desks and lockers. I provided folders for their reading materials, and special containers to hold them. And what about me? I *thought* I was organized. In my second/third grade classroom, the closet was neat and storage boxes labeled. Books were on the shelves, and placed in the correct category. Any books used in planning were always on a bookshelf behind my desk. Student work was usually in a series of cubbies, with each section marked with the subject and grade level. My desk, however, was another story.

I always cleaned off the desk before going home at night, with lesson plans in place and checked papers ready to be handed back to the students. It seemed that as soon as the day started, that neat desktop became cluttered with all kinds of papers and materials. One Friday afternoon I looked at the piles and wrote an inventory in my journal.

One video camera, just used

Power pack for the camera (this dates me)

One video tape, just used

One "Earth Care Annual" which I tried to read while eating lunch at my desk . . . although on the day in question my lunch consisted of a video session in the snow to send to some new pen pals in Texas

Thirty new copies of the *Department of Natural Resources Register*, which were on top of the stapler

One small cassette player with a bird call tape

Four dead AAA batteries from the cassette player

Twenty-one spelling tests, not checked (from the day in question)

One grade book

One lesson plan book-almost ready for next week

Two trade books, used for reading class

Two notebooks, each holding questions and activities for the trade books

Several stones brought in as "gifts" from the playground

One memo book ready for the next week (surprising!)

One empty envelope from popcorn sale money

Three small plastic baskets full of markers, lost pencils (all in need of sharpening), crayons (mostly broken ones), a bottle of white glue someone couldn't open, an old candy cane (thankfully wrapped in plastic), math flashcards and assorted nuts and leaves from our nature trail

Two left over bags of popcorn from that day's sale

One calendar, turned to the correct month

Twenty-three "Scholastic" newspapers for the week, not used

Twenty-three *Tracks* magazines, not used

One set of photographs from the trail

One box of book card lists

One legal pad with a rough draft of a letter to our pen pal teacher

My ballpoint pen (works)

Two note pads (one is never enough)

Two Scotch tape holders (one empty)

A cup with pencils that have "Please Return to Mrs. Labadie" on them

A box of facial tissues, half full (or half empty)

One teacher's bell

Enough already!

Hey! There *is* a desk!!

Rewards of Encouraging Creativity

During my final year of teaching a self-contained classroom of gifted and talented students, I was teaching the fourth and fifth graders that I had taught for two previous years. The students knew me and I knew them. I had heard that sometimes the students could take advantage of the situation, but I wasn't worried about it. I was just concerned that I didn't want to be the same old Mrs. Labadie to the students.

Ken was teaching fifth grade in the same building, and since there was only one classroom of each regular grade, he was pretty much on his own. We decided to change that. He worked with my students for the "Oregon Trail" in social studies, where the students were divided into wagon trains and they had to plan their trip west. Each group experienced hardships such as a lack of drinking water or food, cold, heat, and Indians. Only one "train" made it to Oregon intact. It was a great learning experience in students and teachers working together as well as all the students understanding what the pioneers went through to settle our western territories.

We wanted to get away from the blood and gore of Halloween costumes, so Ken and I decided to ask the students to dress as a historical or literary character. It was rewarding to see that all students in both classrooms followed our suggestion. We had Laura Ingalls Wilder, Indians, and George Washington, to name a few. The students even came up with an activity for the party. They wanted to shell corn by hand! I don't know where they came up with the idea, but it was a great success, and complemented our pioneer studies.

Ken suggested that a special project could be a bird study, which went along well with our nature trail work. The students had to observe at least 20 birds in the wild, draw their pictures, and record where they were sighted and when. These needed to be put into a booklet to turn in. This taught the students not only how to identify birds, but to understand their habitat. It also led to one of my most rewarding experiences in creativity from my students.

April Fool's Day fell on a Friday, and it also happened to be Good Friday. In those days, schools were off on Good Friday. I wasn't expecting any jokes on Thursday, but after the morning recess I noticed a red folder on my desk. It was marked, "Mrs. Labadie." I opened it, and there was a note. "To Mrs. Labadie from her 4th and 5th graders, 1993-1994." Then, another note written on a computer. "Happy April Fool's Day Early." The folder was filled with bird sightings, but the sightings were different than those they had made previously. There was the Football Finch, the Blue J, the Red Dressed Woodpecker, Robin Red Dress, Old Squaw Duck, Western Screech Owl, and the Northern Oreo, to name a few. Documentations were there as to when and where they could be seen, as well as a description of the bird. For example:

The Oreo is a chocolate brown bird with white all around his body. He is commonly mistaken for a cookie.

The Shoe Fly Bird eats flies, dung, and seeds. The bird builds its nest out of shoe laces, leather, hair, and fly wings, lined with soft material. The female shoe fly lays 6 to 8 white or black eggs, spotted with a leathery brown.

The Violet Butting is all violet except his rump is hot pink. They are known for expelling gas. He was sighted in a birdbath washing his butt.

The Red Dressed Woodpecker can be found in any bar in the U.S. "She is one of the best waitresses I've had in a long time," said a bar owner. "She sure brings in the big business." (It was noted that the bird was part bird and part human.)

The Cowbird nests in the field with cows. It eats cow pies. It looks like a cow and has an udder that is hot pink.

And how about the Canadukduk Goose. It is a faint relative of Campbell's Soup and a Canada goose. It resembles a soup can and a goose. It is black and white and also the colors of a soup can. It likes to play duck, duck, goose, and almost always wins. If you look hard enough you might be able to find it in a grocery store in Canada. (Only in Quebec.) Its label is worth more than a million dollars.

The Ring-necked Swan can be seen at elegant parties where there is caviar for him/her to eat. They build their nests out of shiny things like tin foil.

Fiddler Finches are often seen on telephone poles playing country and rock music. They make their nests out of stray fiddle strings. They eat gooseberries and huckleberries.

Each description was accompanied by a drawing of the bird. What a riot! After looking at them and reading every single one, I counted them. There were 55! What creativity. I told the students that I was putting them into a book so that when I was 100 years old I could read them and laugh. Betty added, "You'd better be careful-when you're 100 years old, if you laugh too hard, you'll have a heart attack." What a crew! I did put them into a book and still enjoy reading them. And I believe that creative Betty was the initiator of the project.

This was a reward for me. They took previous learning and used their creative juices and came up with something that they knew I would enjoy. They knew I liked to play with words, and I was thrilled that they learned to do the same. These were "gifted" children, but over the years I learned that all children are capable of being creative if allowed to relax and enjoy their learning.

Smiles, Tears, and Some Unanswered Questions

Rocks and Fossils

An exciting event occurred one November, which influences children (and me) to this very day. Andy and Carson, twins in other classrooms, were sent to me by Andy's teacher, with box in hand. "Mrs. Labadie, we found a dinosaur tooth," was the reason they gave for visiting me.

"Where did you find it? I asked.

They explained the location, which was only about 2 miles from where I lived. They had been following a plow, and it was turned over in the furrow.

Before I even looked, I explained that it wouldn't be a dinosaur tooth—not in Michigan. When I opened the box, I found a beautiful mammoth tooth. I was elated! I immediately took the boys and their find to the office and made a phone call to the local conservation officer, who was great at verifying finds like this one. The officer made a trip to the school, and was as excited as I was. Where we might find a mastodon tooth, mammoth teeth are rare in Michigan. We called the newspaper, and the boys' picture was in two newspapers. I put a protective coating on the tooth, returned it to the boys, and suggested to their mother that she put it in a glass case to protect it from dust.

Many years later the boys donated it to the Elsa Meyer building, where they had attended for several years, and it sits there to this day. I had to clean and repair it, as it was in an open case and was deteriorating. I glued it where it was falling apart, resprayed it with a preservative, and bought a nice glass case with a glass top to keep it clean. It's in the school library, so all can see it. What a nice contribution to the Corunna schools, and an exciting story for the boys (now men), to tell their grandchildren.

Several years after the boys found their tooth, I visited one of our teachers, who had just given birth to her first baby. Teresa said she had something to show me—that in excavating for the basement, what appeared to be a tooth was found. Yes, it was a tooth—this time a mastodon tooth. I was thrilled. I took the tooth to the Ruthven Museum in Ann Arbor (this was before I became really involved with paleontology at the museum). The paleontologist took the tooth up to a mastodon that was on display and showed me where the tooth sat in the animal's mouth. I wrote the information down and returned the tooth and the data to Teresa. She keeps the tooth in a box in her classroom closet, and shares it with her students whenever appropriate. I also borrow it when I share my fossils in her building. Her students are always excited to see the treasure and hear the story. No wonder I am always looking for treasures like these when I am near any digging!

During the teaching of a unit on Geology, I usually included a favorite topic of the students, Prehistoric Life. The students enjoyed learning about the Geologic Time Scale, and when different types of life appeared and became extinct. The students would work in groups and come up with dioramas, murals, plays, and present findings of the different time periods to the class. Of course, they loved reading about dinosaurs. I had a "dinosaur license" that gave the student permission to find a dinosaur and bring it to school. There were strict rules, however. If they found a T-Rex, for example, it had to be a male, and had to be on a leash. The student was allowed to keep it for only one day. The students got quite a kick out of the license, and at least one student and her father took the license to heart.

A few days after receiving the license, in walked Jenny and her father, pulling a 4 foot inflatable T-Rex on a dolly, with a leash around his neck. Talk about creative!! I kept that dinosaur and took it to school every year. Even when I was a principal, I had "Dino" in my office. In fact, after about 15 years, there are times I still carry him to schools when I teach classes about dinosaurs. However, he is not alone. I now have a girl T-Rex named Roxie. When it's her turn to visit a school, I put a bow on her head. One year a little boy came into the room and immediately said, "She's a girl!" Someone asked him how he knew, and he answered, "She's wearing a bow!" Don't we have fun?

I brought in fossils for the kids to work with. They wore goggles and used dental picks and had a ball trying to extract the fossils from matrix. I had created a latex mold of a trilobite so they could create their own cast out of plaster. I also gave them several fossils to keep. While passing these "goodies" out, the kids spontaneously broke out in the song, *For She's a Jolly Good Fellow*. After it was over, someone piped up, "We should have sung, For she's a jolly good fossil!" I laughed and said, "Thanks, but it's okay."

Another fossil project that I had been doing was bringing in tailings from a phosphate mine. Each kid received a cup full to look through. They found tiny shark teeth, small coprolites, (they loved the "poop"), small vertebrae, and fish bones. Of course, they could keep what they found, and all were thrilled with their treasures.

Years later, I received a letter from Alan. He was in the Navy in the south, and talked about responding to a question as to whether he had ever acted in a play. His response? "I proclaimed myself a professional from my experiences in The Wizard of Oz, Alice in Wonderland and The Prince and the Pauper." It was right after that discussion that he received a newspaper clipping from his mother telling how I was going into classrooms sharing about fossils and fossil hunting. He included a picture of himself with the letter (in which he shared about his life), and told me to "Show this in your fossil display from the Paleolithic section of history." He never lost his sense of humor.

One year I "adopted" a new teacher who was teaching a classroom of cognitively impaired students. She needed a mentor, so she and I frequently worked together a lot—she with her students, and I with my "gifted" students. I went into her classroom to teach about rocks and fossils, and was rewarded the next day when Terry brought me a large rock as a gift. I was thrilled, of course. He was so proud of my response that the next day he brought me an entire bag. The next day another bag came in, and I had to tell him that I had enough rocks. He laughed, and several years later, upon seeing me at the middle school, asked if I remembered all the rocks he gave me. Did I remember? Oh, yes. I was using the large one in my garden!

Party Happenings

During my first year of teaching in Bloomingdale we had an unusual Christmas party. It seems during the night before the party the people in the small town were awakened by a large "boom" coming from the school. The boiler in the elementary school had blown up. There was no great damage to the school, but of course there was no heat, and it was cold and snowy. No Christmas party? The administration decided we couldn't do without it, so they brought the students in as usual and took them to the high school gym. The teachers and parents gathered all the presents and took them and the food to the gym where tables had been arranged around the perimeter. Over 200 students, kindergarten through sixth grade were all partying in the gym at the same time. The students were excited, but well behaved. A "different" party, but what a lot of fun. After 2 hours the students were taken home, all ready for the holiday break. The break also allowed for the boiler to be replaced, and school opened on time in January.

In years gone by the school used to bus the students to special places for end of the year parties. When I had Dan as a third grader, we went to the beef cattle ranch where he lived and which his father managed for a large conglomerate. The students were treated to a hay ride and were taken to the cutting area where one of the ranch hands demonstrated how a cutting horse "cuts" a steer out of a herd. It was something new for all of us to observe. After a tour of the entire ranch, we had grilled hamburgers made out of their own beef. Trips like that helped give the students a sense of community. Unfortunately, the next year the ranch was closed and the family moved east, where Dan's father managed another, bigger ranch.

With budget cuts the school discontinued the trips, so we usually went to our trail, slid down the slopes of the cliffs nearby on large pieces of cardboard, and picked and ate wild strawberries.

There were still ways to have parties, though. I worked with all 3 children of Ken Black and his wife Janice, and they were always a big help with support on our trail and on the trip to Canada while hunting fossils. One year they planned a Saturday party at their home, and most of the students and their parents attended. They had a pond and the students loved to ride in the paddle boat and explore the nature that surrounded the home. These special days helped create a school family, and I always felt a big part of that family.

A Difficult Year

Was I ever discouraged? Absolutely. During an early year of teaching I had a difficult class of twenty boys and nine girls. There was every kind of problem that would come to a teacher's mind. Two boys would sneak downtown at noon and were caught stealing. Then they would sneak to the high school at noon. Why did they have so much "free" time? In those days schools had over an hour for lunch because some children walked home to eat. Suspensions of elementary students were rare, and it all fell on the teacher to work with the problems.

Another boy lost his parents and two siblings in a drunk driver accident. He was one of six children orphaned. All the surviving children were enveloped in love by the mother's sister, who had recently married. The entire school community came together to assist this family in their time of grief and reorganization.

Hyperactivity was a problem even in the 1960s. I had one boy who was impulsive; hitting, laughing at others, fighting. He had seen his mother killed, which had put a mental strain on his young life. I wrote in my journal,

"I think I have failed with J. I haven't seen any success." We had no special education, no counselors, no one to help me. What a tragedy for him. There were many days when I'd come home from school in tears, and question my being a teacher. It was an emotionally trying year for me. I wrote:

"As I look back on this past year, I see many mistakes I've made, as well as what I've done right. I realize this class had been a difficult one even in kindergarten, because of the mix of different personalities. I only hope I have had SOME positive influence on them."

Wasn't there ANY success that year? Sure. These were wonderful children whom I loved despite my tears, and as I reflected, I saw a lot of growth in me. Growth in helping to understand students' problems and how these problems affect their entire lives. I learned how important a teacher is to the students, even though their time at school is short. I saw how important the integration of programs for special needs students was. Miss Crampton had also said there would be times like this. It's a part of teaching and growing.

More Smiles and Unanswered Questions

There was always something spontaneous happening, and it wasn't always about rocks or fossils. One day Paul brought in an old 78 rpm record, "The Emperor Waltz." I can't remember the significance of the record, but we talked about the differences in record speed (This was long before CDs). I then played the waltz, and proceeded to waltz around the room. Immediately the kids got up and joined in. Boys with boys and girls with girls, but we all danced.

Different cultures brought up many questions. An exchange student from Japan visited us, and the students were delighted. She was asked what her religion was, and she said she had no religion. The students didn't question her any further on the subject, but later we had quite a discussion. How could she get married if she doesn't go to church? Will she go to heaven? How can she believe there is no God? We discussed the legal aspects of marriage, and I told the students that as for heaven, we'd have to wait to find out.

Some of the teachers were "coaches" for after school basketball games for the third, fourth and fifth graders. Of course, I helped. I know I'm not a great basketball player, but the kids do the work and the coach cheers them on.

We usually had a teacher vs. student basketball game to finish out the season. In previous years the coaches made crazy mistakes just so the kids could win. It was becoming harder, though, and we had to work just to look like we wanted to win. (Now, it couldn't be that we were aging, could it?) Jan, mother of one of my students, said to me after the teacher/student game my last year, "It's a good thing you can make money teaching, because you sure wouldn't make it playing basketball!" I laughed. What a friend! And I even made 2 baskets!

On the last day of school that same year one student and her father presented me with a nice trophy with "To the World's Greatest Teacher" engraved on it. I was pleasantly surprised, and still have it in my office at home. I wonder, though, maybe this was the trophy I would never get playing basketball?

I will always remember Leland. I first saw him when, as a preschooler, he came with his mother to pick up his older sister. He wore a cowboy hat, cowboy boots, and had a holster and cap guns. He was in his own little world, and ran around playing cowboys. I thought, "Egad, that is some kid." Later, Leland, with his bright red hair and blue eyes, was in my third grade classroom. I soon found out he certainly was "some kid." He was creative, was quite an artist, was determined to succeed and didn't mind working for it, had a quick wit, friendly personality and a ready smile. I chuckle at my thoughts of first seeing him, and am thankful that I had a chance to work with him.

Jeff and Bob were talking in the bus line. Jeff felt Bob's arm muscle (Bob was as thin as a rail.) and said, "Wow! You're not even flexing it!" Bob, of course, was all smiles. Then Jeff added, "But it was a little flabby." Bob was crushed, but Jeff reassured him that he had great muscles. He knew how to be diplomatic after all.

There had been a TV special on volcanoes that aired over the weekend. Many of the students had watched it, so a class discussion ensued. The kids were fascinated by how islands were formed from them and why they suddenly erupt. I spoke about pressure cookers and teakettles to get across the idea. Toni finally got it. She suggested it was like "throwing up." She said it had to come up, and there was no stopping it. Perfect analogy, Toni.

These television specials were important to all of us. I watched one, called "The World We Never See," on tiny creatures that live in the water as well as larger land animals that live underground, as moles. The narrator stated, "Anyone who has gone swimming in a lake has swallowed thousands of animals, such as copepods, without harm."

Larry did not like that idea. I told him they would not live in us, but would be killed by the acids in one's stomach. He added, "Yeah, but they'd tickle."

We were reading about mythology, and I read from a cartoon type booklet about Nasnays—a half man, split down the center. The story said he hopped on his one leg around the deserts, and the drawing showed him as a side view without clothes. This caused quite a stir, and we decided we knew who the world's first "streaker" was.

Jason came up to me after recalling a discussion on recycling and conservation. He and Marty had been taking down pictures on a bulletin board, and he held out his hand to show me that he had saved all the staples. He asked if they could be recycled. I told him it was possible, but it sure would take a lot of staples to make a load for the recycling center.

Kenny and I were reading a book about pythons and anacondas one day, when we came to a picture where a python had eaten an entire wild pig. Of course, the snake's middle was swollen enormously. Kenny said, "And I thought peanut butter went down hard." Then, Daniel found another picture where a python had eaten a goat. He said, "I wonder if the horns stuck out of him." The boys were so fascinated. And how interesting to me to let them question and try to figure things out.

Once, after watching a movie with Marlo Thomas, called "Free To Be—You and Me," I talked about working toward a goal in college. I told them they should not give up future plans because of money. College could be financed in many ways . . . and so on. Janice said, "Gee—you sound just like the man at church!" Yes, call me Reverend!

I had been concerned about Mariette. She was a bright girl, and a little immature, but there seemed to be no reason for the poor quality of her work. One day she spelled all the answers wrong on a reading assignment, and they were all on the paper in a list. I asked her why, and after thinking for a minute, she said, "My mother hit me in the head, and I just haven't been thinking straight." I gave her a good talking to, and also talked to her mother, and I never heard any more about her head.

During my first few years of teaching I had two accidents in which boys broke their teeth on the ice. We never allowed sliding on ice during recesses, but both happened when the boys were playing around before school started. Once, in Wisconsin, Robin came in with a bloody mouth. He had fallen when sliding and his mouth hit his metal lunch box. A permanent front tooth was badly chipped. Mother came in and he was taken to get a cap. The other incident happened in Bloomingdale. Keith was also playing on the ice and fell. His fall caused such bad chips on both his beautiful front teeth that he was taken to the dentist, also for caps. However, his caps were full sized and silver. I think his family was happy that school pictures were taken before this happened. The memories of these accidents were always with me, and I was really firm about the kids staying off the ice at school. I know I was a "pain" to the custodians, in that I was fussy about salt being placed on real icy spots. There was a good reason!

Of course students are curious, and I always encouraged it. However, when you have a cactus plant in the classroom you tell the students "Hands off!" Marlene came over to me one day and complained of pains on one of her fingers. She said that whenever she touched something, it hurt. I looked closely, and not seeing anything, I took out a magnifying glass. There were tiny white cactus spines on her finger. I asked her where she had been and she related that she had just been standing by the window. When asked if she had touched the cactus, guilt overcame her, and she quietly admitted that she had. I explained what she had in her finger, and gave her the magnifying glass and tweezers. She and another student when to the back of the room and pulled out all the spines. That was a lesson well learned.

While discussing bicycle safety, we talked about accidents between cars and bikes. Susan offered, "My dad has never run over a kid on a bike, but he sure did run over a skunk."

We had the annual vision and hearing screenings. Katie, the eye technician, had been coming to our building for years, and we enjoyed having her work with our kids. I had told her that these kids were EXCELLENT in bringing their glasses to school. I don't think I ever had to nag anyone about it. When I reminded them to take their glasses to the screening, Julie and Sue both said, "Uh, oh!" I asked, half laughingly, "What? And I told Mrs. B that you were so good at remembering them!" Kendra added, "Well, guess we proved your hypothesis wrong." Now where did she learn that?

One March we planted petunia seeds so they could be transplanted to the front of the building later in the spring. Jeremy's mother brought in rich topsoil to mix with the potting soil I had. Most of the kids were outside for recess, but Jeremy and Peter stayed inside to help mix the two together in a large bucket. As the boys dove in with both hands, Jeremy said, "We have good soil. We get it from the manure pile."

Peter's hands quickly came out of the bucket. He brushed them off, and put them behind his back. I laughingly said, "What's the matter, Peter, don't you want to help now that you know where the dirt came from?"

He answered, "Yeah," and laughed. But, he did get his hands into the dirt later while planting, and enjoyed telling the rest of the class about the source of the rich soil. I still chuckle when I think about it, and when I see bags of manure being sold in the stores.

On Being a "Bag Lady"

For one year I was considered a "bag lady." After the many years of teaching gifted and talented students in a self contained classroom, I spent time in each of the three elementary buildings working with identified students in a pull-out situation, and "pushing into" their classrooms to teach to the entire group in the room. The identified students were clustered into one classroom per grade, but I also worked with other classrooms so students wouldn't feel left out.

Scheduling was difficult. It meant being in grades two through five in each building at a time that was workable for each teacher. I also had to substitute teach occasionally, which meant my meetings with the students was canceled for the day. It was also difficult to find a meeting place. In my regular building, a small room attached to my "office" off the library served as our primary location, but in the other buildings I was moved from place to place, depending on what was available. I kept smiling, though, and was sure to thank the principals for finding me a spot. They really did their best to help me.

I bought a set of "wheels" onto which I fastened a plastic tub. This helped carry the many items I needed to take in to work with the various grade levels. The wheels and tub were most helpful, but in the winter they acted like a snowplow, and I was pushing show all the way to the outside door or to my van. I always carried a planner. Flexibility was the key, because I wasn't usually told in advance about special assemblies or other events that could be a priority in a certain building.

In this way I was able to work with more students, and grew to know the teachers better than I had before. They welcomed me into their classrooms, and I loved being in them. A fourth grade boy came to me one day, gave me a hug, and asked me if I was going to "drag into" the classroom or "push out" the students. Obviously, he meant, "push in" or "pull out."

In the same building a first grader saw me in the hall and said, "Good morning," and gave me a hug. I said "Good morning; and how are you today?" He answered, "I'm fine. And what have you been up to lately?" I told him I had been working with students, and he replied with an "Oh," and headed to the office. And I didn't even work with the first graders!

Another comment came from a boy not in my buildings, or even in our school system. Bob was my neighbor, and knew I was working with fossils with some of the classes. He told his cousin that I was an "alientologist." Was I alien? Possibly.

The following year when I was a principal, I was working in my office after school when a voice asked, "Mrs. Labadie, may I use the phone?"

I called out, "I don't know. Who is this?"

"It's one of your cluster kids!"

I went into the outer office and found a fifth grader who had been in one of my "push in" classrooms. She hadn't been one of my "identified" students, but I was genuinely pleased that she considered herself one of "my kids." Yes, I thought all of them important, and she knew it. That was proof that the program was effective for all students.

I enjoyed the "bag lady routine," but it did get to be old fast. Probably one thing that kept me going was my coursework at Michigan State University, where I was working on administrative certification. I knew I wasn't going to do this job forever. However, I also knew I would miss being in every building and working with all the teachers. They were wonderful for accepting my ideas and me. I became close to teachers that I had never worked with before.

The position also gave me time to compare the organization of each building and to check out the relationships (or lack of) between the principals and the staff. This was a blessing for the next position I was to hold. We hired another teacher to continue the position of coordinator of the gifted and talented program after I was accepted as a principal for one of the elementary buildings. I had taught in the program since its inception in 1978, and had moved with the changes. I knew it was time for new blood.

The Role of Principal

I was excited about my new role. I prepared my office lovingly, with artifacts gathered on fossil hunts, and two animal skulls, a deer and a raccoon. I worked many summer hours in order to be ready for fall.

Many of the responsibilities of being a principal are confidential. Therefore, my journaling was never kept up to the extent that I would have liked. However, I did write down many things that a reader might find interesting and/or humorous.

The younger students kept confusing Linda, the secretary, and me. We did not look alike, but when they'd come up to us and call us the wrong name, we'd say, "That's okay. It's because we look so much alike." The students would usually agree.

One day Linda was out of the office. A little first grader came up to me and said, "I'd like to see the principal."

"I'm the principal. Can I help you?"

"No, I want to talk to the *other* principal." Laughingly, I went to get Linda. She was known from that time on as the "other principal."

The little guys did not know what the principal did. They didn't see me working. They usually saw me when I was greeting them in the morning, checking on the lunchroom, making one of my frequent stops in their classrooms, or seeing them onto the buses after school. When they came to the office they usually saw Linda working. So, it was understandable for them to think that she was the principal.

Early in my tenure as principal, Cindy, a little pre-first grader was in tears. She "missed her mommy." I took her to the office where I could take time to talk to her. A second grader, Cathy, was sitting in the lobby because she had broken her collarbone and couldn't go out for noon recess. Cathy offered to help Cindy by reading to her. Cathy put her arm around Cindy and sat her down next to her. The two looked at books and talked. Cindy told Cathy that she "had never gone to "all days" before. When Cathy had to go back to class,

I started to take Cindy to the lunchroom. I also asked her if she'd like to talk to her older sister, who was in another classroom in the building. She answered, "No, she's in class and I really shouldn't disturb her." So grown up and yet so young. At that point her teacher came along and Cindy joined her class at lunch. And you know, there were never tears again.

Terry was a little boy from China who spoke little English. He was quiet and spoke very little outside of the classroom. Every morning I greeted him as he got off the bus, and every afternoon I told him goodbye as he boarded the bus. During the day I spoke to him whenever I could, but I don't recall him ever talking directly to me. Of course, we don't know what the little guys must be thinking in their own language.

Terry's adjustment was slow, but he really came around during his second year. It was after I retired when I stopped in to congratulate Jenny, a para-pro who had been nominated as "employee of the month." Terry's classroom was having ice cream floats in Jenny's honor, and his teacher invited me in for the party. I sat near Terry and some other children. Terry looked at me and asked, "Is that your real hair?" I almost fell off my chair. Is that what he was thinking all last year? I said, "Yes. Do you want to touch it?" He did. His family was young, all with the straight black hair we see on persons of Chinese descent. My hair was silver, wavy, and short. Though I was surprised, I was pleased that he felt he could talk to me. What progress!

During those years as principal I spent many hours in the health room, and a lot of them were checking for head lice. When we saw "epidemics" we did checks of entire rooms. The kids enjoyed the checks, and joked about them. One kindergartner told me that we wouldn't find any bugs in his hair. When I asked why, he said, "Because they're sleeping." Another kindergartner asked if we were checking for "head lights."

Linda was pretty good at spotting the nits, but she said she had never seen an adult. Well, I found them, and could even catch them. Often I would put one in a plastic bag to show the parents if they insisted there weren't any. Once in a while the kids were interested in seeing what was in their hair. I brought a microscope to the office for them to check the critters out. How interesting! Linda then became pretty good at spotting the fast little adults also.

There were times we didn't get much help from parents on lice. One set of grandparents who were raising two granddaughters, had to come to school to pick one of them up because after seeing her scratching her head, the teacher sent her to the office. Sure enough, lice. When Grandpa arrived, he was irate. He told me that we needed to close the school until WE got the problem under control. He called the superintendent's office and told them that the lice were there when school opened, and we should close the building down. He kept both girls out for three days. I was surprised but pleased that they did work on the girls' hair despite his blaming us.

We had our share of accidents. I must admit that Linda was the queen of first aid. When a student was brought in with an obviously broken arm, she took right over. While she handled the girl, I tried calling her parents. The girl told me that her mother was in Grand Rapids at a conference, and her father was sleeping. (He worked nights.) When I couldn't get an answer on the phone, she said that he wore earplugs. I hopped into my trusty Durango and headed for the house, which was less than a mile away. There was no response to my knocks and calling at the door. Though how I got into the house is a secret known only to the family and me, I managed to enter the house and called. I went to the stairway and called. Nothing. There was a door off the kitchen that was closed. I knocked and called. A very stunned and sleepy father roused and said loudly, "What?" I talked to him through the door and told him what had happened. He said that he would meet us at the hospital.

When I arrived back at the school, the ambulance was already there. The girl had become pale, and Linda and the physical education teacher suspected that she might go into shock. I followed the ambulance and stayed with her until her father arrived. That was one time I was glad I had the nerve to enter someone's house without permission. And yes, the parents were also thankful.

Another interesting accident was when two boys were brought in from the playground—one with a badly chipped front tooth, and another with a slightly bleeding head. It seems they collided—and it must have been quite a hit, because the broken tooth from the one boy was stuck in the gash in the other boy's head.

We always hear how kids swallow things they shouldn't, and put things up their noses. Well, we had both. One second grader swallowed a quarter. His mother picked him up and took him to have an x-ray. The coin had to be surgically removed, as it was already lodging in the base of the stomach.

And then there was the little kindergartner who was brought into the office because he told the teacher he had put a little stone up his nose. Another pick-up by a worried mother, and a check and removal by the doctor. It was a troublesome removal for the child, but he was back in school the next day.

Besides the usual head lice, ringworm and chicken pox, there were some very traumatic events in those years. One student was in treatment for a tumor that was not malignant, and another student was treated for one that was. Two mothers were treated for cancer, one of who survived and is healthy today. Another mother was in an automobile accident and was comatose for several weeks. She finally came home after nine weeks, but it took a long time for her mobility to come back. Another mother and her first grader were in an accident and the child had to jump out of the broken window. With his bloodied face he had to run to a house for help. The boy was called a hero, and rightly so. He had many stitches and scabs on his face, but healed quickly.

I remember one time that the social climate was hot from two cases of sexual abuse, one of physical abuse, and a nasty custody fight between parents, neither of whom was fit to be a parent in my eyes. That year I grew to know the caseworkers from the county on a first name basis. I had heard stories where they would not show up for days, but that was not my experience. They were always there when called, and I was thankful for them.

One morning one of our buses was run off the road and into a ditch. Some of our students and parents waiting for the bus at an apartment complex saw the accident and called 911. The driver also had her radio and called for help. The students were taken off in pouring rain and brought to school by other buses. One girl and the driver were taken to the hospital to be checked. I had to talk to each student to make sure they were okay, and then call every parent to let them know what had happened, in case they heard a report and were worried about their child. Though I only had 15 students on the bus at the time, the day was hectic. But as I reflected on it, I didn't have a single discipline problem in the office. It turned out to be a good day after all!

We had a couple of humorous events with wild animals. One fall day I was working at my desk when I spotted a doe and two young deer (probably from the spring's birthing) walk across the kick-ball field. As I watched, the doe and one of the youngsters cut through a row of trees and disappeared. The other obviously hungry deer walked along the row of trees to where some shrubs were growing. I couldn't see the berries, but it's possible there were some on the branches. He stood on his hind legs, supported himself on the wire fence and nibbled away. It wasn't long before the doe returned and watched him. Finally, just like an exasperated mother, she went to him and nosed his back. The young deer stopped, looked at her and then continued eating. She pushed at him again, and he relented and followed her. That was just like a child, I thought.

Another time some children came in from the playground and said that a raccoon was near the swings. Now why was a raccoon on a playground with noisy children in the middle of the day? I went to look and sure enough, there he was. He was wandering all around, with the curious children watching and laughing. After making sure the playground aide was keeping an eye out for the safety of the children, I returned to the office and called the sheriff's office, in order to have animal control come out. They were there right away, and took a net onto the playground. The raccoon headed for the nearby field and woods. The officers looked at me strangely, like I was crazy. "He'll stay away now," they said. "He might have just been disoriented." As they started walking toward their vehicles, the raccoon headed back to the playground, possibly intent on using the climbing bars for exercise. The surprised officers scurried around, chased the critter, and finally captured it in the net. They put it in a cage and headed out. We were all happy that he would be examined and if healthy would be released in a safe area.

One of the most emotionally draining events was with Charles. Charles was in the children's intensive care ward of Children's Hospital at the University of Michigan. He was diagnosed with primary pulmonary hypertension, and would need to wear a heart catheter and use oxygen. This was caused by a genetic defect that had slowly progressed to the point his custodial grandparents sought help. Before he returned to school we brought together a team including his grandmother, the teacher, the teacher aides who would be working with him, and an ambulance crew. He needed an oxygen tank at school. We arranged for him to ride a special education bus so he'd have a shorter ride without oxygen. The tanks weren't allowed on the buses unless they were bolted down, and his regular bus was crowded. We didn't want to take a chance on the catheter becoming dislodged or his computer that operated it being hit. He couldn't go out for recess for fear of being hit. His participation in gym was of course, nil. The most frightening part was that if something happened to his catheter, CPR would do no good.

At first some of the staff was hesitant to have him in school. Knowing the law, I remained firm that he would attend. Thankfully, his teacher, Karen, and his grandmother prepared the children for his arrival, and the year progressed nicely and without incident. It was difficult for him to even go to the park (two blocks away) with the class. I either took him in my car with his tank, or if he needed to ride the bus, I would follow with the oxygen in my car. One of the aides was assigned to hook him up to the oxygen every morning and put the tank away each night. In fact, the teachers, once they understood the way we would handle the monitoring, all pulled together to support Charles.

Yes, we adults felt sorry for him, but Charles was a fighter. He was always cheerful and had a positive attitude. Academically he was doing excellent work. What an example he set for all of us. Sometimes adults need a role model, and even a child can be that model.

By the time Charles was in middle school he was off oxygen during the day. That alone was a miracle. He had fought to have the energy to ride his bike again, and had a portable oxygen pack that he used. The exercise probably helped build up his lungs. He truly was our miracle boy.

And oh, boy. Those pre-first graders were hilarious. Sandy brought a little guy down to the office so he could tell me a joke that his dad told him.

"The first little pig went into a restaurant, ordered some food, asked where the bathroom was, and left. The second little pig went into the restaurant, ordered some food, asked where the bathroom was, and left. The third little pig went into the restaurant, ordered some food, and was about to leave when the waitress asked him, 'Don't you want to know where the bathroom is?' The little pig said, 'Don't you know the story of the three little pigs? I'm the one that went "Wee Wee Wee" all the way home." I admit, I cracked up. The little guy probably didn't remember his letters, but he remembered the joke.

One day three little first graders were sent in. I asked them what had happened, and they said that one of them said he'd throw the others in the garbage. I told them "If you aren't careful, I'll throw all of you in the garbage." They looked at me seriously, and I grinned. They laughed. Then we got down to their escapades. It seems that one was opening the door on the side of the dumpster. The others said that they weren't opening it, but shutting it. I told them they were not to be near the dumpster. After a little scolding, I took them into the hall and told them to wait for their classes, which were coming in from the playground. I heard some talking and laughing, so I went back, glared at them, and said gently but firmly, "Now, zip it!" and one of the little guys automatically grabbed at his pants zipper. I added, "your lips." They stopped talking and stood. I went into the office, almost unable to contain myself.

Kindergartners were so spontaneous. While on one of my classroom walk-throughs, I went into the kindergarten room, where the teacher had been working with writing numbers up to 20. The numbers were still on the board, and she asked the kids to write them on paper without looking. She and I walked around, and saw one little boy writing with his eyes closed. You guessed it! He wasn't looking!

Gifts were always brought to the principal's office—like a bouquet of milkweed pods from first graders, or rocks that looked like fossils. The children knew my interest in fossils and nature, and were anxious to please me. Love it!

It was always a joy to see the middle school students stop in to say hello. Don had been quite a peeler, but he had personality plus. He had problems on the bus, along with his younger brother, and both spent time in the office explaining what was going on. Don was always honest with me, and I believe he worked hard to prevent problems. We enjoyed talking about fossils, Nascar, and other things that kids are interested in. He was also the hero of the automobile accident as a little guy. One day he stopped in while I was dismissing the students. He gave me a hug and said, "I really miss you, Mrs. Labadie."

I responded with, "I miss you, too, Don."

"No," he added. "I mean I REALLY miss you!"

Now that's a reward!

I was once taking a class in administration from Michigan State University, and teachers had been invited to talk about their views of administration. One teacher said, "I don't want to be a principal because I love the kids too much."

I responded with, "Don't you want a principal who loves the kids?"

The talk with Don only shows that a principal who shows the kids that they really care—that they love them, even when the kids get in trouble, receives love and respect in return.

Ben had entered kindergarten but it was obvious from day one that he was not ready, so we transferred him into the pre-school program, located in a different building. His older brother was in our building, so it was easy to keep in touch. The following year Ben was brought back into our kindergarten class. On one of my visits after I retired he spotted me while in his first grade classroom. He told his teacher, "Mrs. Labadie and I go back a long way!"

The following year Ben's mother died, and without a father in the picture, he went to live with his grandmother. At the funeral home I talked to his brother, but Ben had left for the afternoon. I often think of him, and wonder how he is doing.

Through the years the loss of students has always troubled me. I told my staff, to **"Love the kids while you have them, because you don't know what their future will be. We are a small part of their lives, and if you make one little dent in their life, it is worth it. Maybe they won't even remember-but the impact will still be there."**

Remembering some troubling days when I was a child, I also told them that I didn't want to see any child humiliated or discriminated against because of who the parents were, what they wore or how much money they had. Being from a large family where financial problems were frequent, I was often made fun of, and I didn't want any child to go through humiliations. That had always been one of my missions as a teacher, and I wanted my staff to know my mission.

I was not a real "heavy" of a principal, but some of the teachers said that when I went into their classrooms for formal observations, they were really nervous. One new teacher was certainly not afraid of me. Sam was 6'7" and gave me something to look up to. He was a neat guy, though, and worked hard—usually. One day I was in his classroom to teach about Native Americans. I had many artifacts, and enjoyed sharing them with the kids. As I was talking, I looked at Sam, who was at the back of the room, sawing logs. When I finished my lesson, I laughingly told him I would get even with him. Another teacher was in on the secret, and made sure I remembered to follow through. During Sam's formal observation, I sat at the back of the room writing. Then, I leaned my head back on the chalkboard and pretended to sleep. He was shocked at first, but soon caught on to my ruse. We both still laugh at the experience.

Second graders composed a book for me on Principal's Day. It states,

"Mrs. Labadie is very nice. Mrs. Labadie helps the school. Mrs. Labadie is the boss of the school.

Mrs. Labadie keeps track of our school. Our school's name is Elsa Meyer.

Mrs. Labadie takes care of us. Mrs. Labadie is nice to us. She is a nice lady.

I like her because she is nice. We are very nice to her because we know that she is a good principal. I like Mrs. Labadie because she likes butterflies and I do too.

Mrs. Labadie likes the kids. She helps us by watching over us. She never wants to quit her job."

No, I never wanted to quit my job. I will never quit. I just move on. So, after 5 glorious years of administration, I applied to Michigan State University to work in the Teacher Education Department. I was offered the job, so I retired from Corunna after 37 years in public schools. People were good to me. The newspaper had a great article, titled, "Principal has unique idea of retirement" because I had stated that I would also be continuing my volunteer work at the University of Michigan Museum of Paleontology. I have saved cards and letters, and most of all, a quilt that the students made.

The quilt was amazing. Every student decorated a block and one was chosen from each room to go on the quilt. They were transferred to muslin squares. The staff put their handprints on the back. And you know, not one out of the 400+ students spilled the beans. The main reason the quilt was special is stated in the Epilogue, "Full Circle."

Another surprise was during the dress rehearsal for the final music performance of the year, the music director dedicated the singing of "You're a Grand Old Flag" to me. When my students had performed the play on the constitution, we sang several songs from George M. Cohan, and they are favorites of mine. The song meant a lot to me. Thank you, students, and Mr. D.

I am invited back to teach about fossils, to help with the French Voyageur Encampment and the eighth grade History Day. For the encampment I serve as a guide on the walkway along the river, and I show the students different plants and tell how the Native Americans and early settlers used them. On the History Day I am a docent in one of the historical buildings in the Historical Village. I must admit that these little side "jobs" keep me learning new things. One of the joys of helping out is to see the kids as they grow up, especially since I am not a regular visitor in the school buildings. And do we really want to quit. I don't think so.

My silver hair gives me a natural grandmotherly look, where children are not afraid of me. A trip after my retirement to give materials to a teacher, found former students in the hall giving me lots of hugs. The little pre-first graders had eaten lunch and were on their way outside. It had been "Beach Day," in the lunchroom, so the kids wore shorts, etc., and had sat on blankets while eating sack lunches. Some of these students had come from another building, so were not familiar to me. That didn't bother one little guy. He came up to me, held up the legs to his pants, and asked, "Would you help me put my legs back on?" He was wearing pants with zipper legs, and needed to put them back on in order to go outside in the chilly air. We finally got them in place and zipped up, and out he scampered. You know, I really do miss those little ways to help kids.

I must admit that some administrators put parents as one of the stresses of the job. Not me. I enjoyed the parents, and am grateful that they supported the school, the entire staff, and me. Most importantly, the parents supported their children.

The staff was outstanding in their work with the students. They were dedicated and were always there to help when needed, whether it was monitoring students when buses were late, during assemblies, or in working with special needs students. We worked as a team; custodians, aides, secretaries, cooks and certified staff. **They** were what made the school the "best" in the county, and my job possible and enjoyable.

Except, that is, when a poor teacher was involved. It was so difficult to place students in a classroom where the teacher was not effective, and where the kids hated to come to school. It was difficult to prove ineffectiveness, as when I would walk in, all would be well. It was saying that either the kids or the teacher was lying. It was "he said, she said," and dismissal of a tenured teacher is tough. That's a case where a teacher was given tenure when it should not have been given. Many of us (staff, parents, kids), could breathe a sigh of relief at certain retirements.

How do we know when to leave a job? Principals and teachers alike should not be afraid to retire. We need to leave before we become stale. Before the kids "get to" us. Leave when you are a success. Now be assured that I didn't say, "quit." There is a difference.

I moved to the university level because I felt my job was done. The school was moving along nicely and it was time to let a new, younger principal in. The staff needed some new ideas and fresh leadership. Was I sad? Yes. And I miss not being directly involved in the events. However, time moves on. And I moved on to helping new teachers learn the profession. Did I quit, second graders? No. I just moved along. The journey of a teacher never ends.

Epilogue

Full Circle

You hear about things coming "full circle," but what does that really mean? On my final week as principal I scheduled an awards assembly for the first and second grades in the morning, and for the third through fifth grades in the afternoon. Some of the fifth graders also received a Presidential Academic Award, so parents and other family members had been invited.

After the presidential awards had been passed out, I directed the award-winning students to go outside for pictures. Before they could leave the gym the younger students came trooping in, and several entered the west door with a quilt in their hands. Every student in the school (over 400) had made pictures highlighting my years as principal, and one picture from every classroom had been selected to be put on a muslin quilt block. A bright blue "teacher" print framed the blocks. Staff handprints had been put on the backing of muslin (And might I add that not one student "leaked" the surprise.)

Probably the most memorable square was that from the pre-first grade. I learned to love the spontaneity of these little guys, but I also knew that they were very literal. What did they choose for a quilt square? A lot of squares, one inside the other!

This has been the most emotional part of my retirement. I reflected to the audience that when I was kindergarten, my teacher had made muslin curtains. We children colored pictures on them, and she ironed them so the pictures would stay. I don't remember what picture I made, but those curtains have been a vivid memory for my entire life. I never forgot how I would sit at the table and gaze at their beauty. How appropriate to receive a quilt made of muslin blocks, colored by students, which resembled the muslin drawings of my childhood. The beginning of my public school experience and the end.